Little Acorn Books

About Early Writing

EARLY WRITING SKILLS PRACTICE FUN

by Marilynn G. Barr

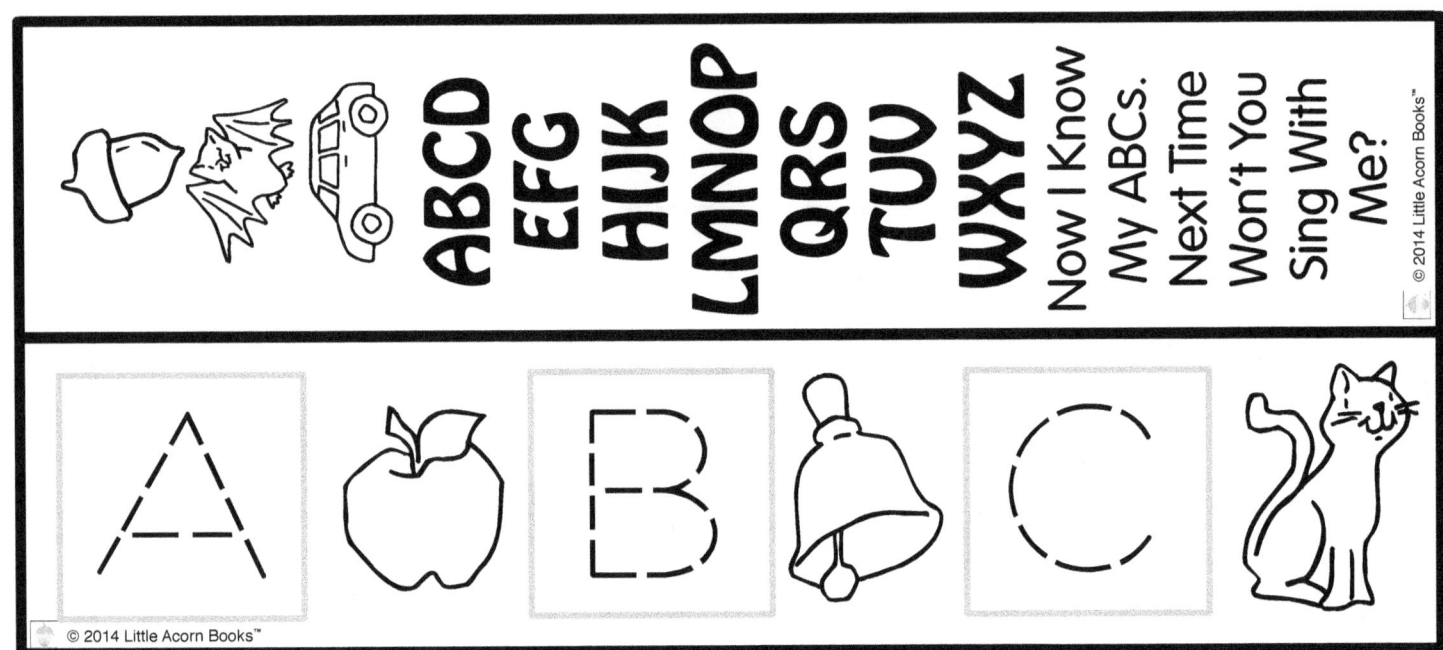

LAB20148P
ABOUT WRITING MATH
Early Writing Skills Practice Fun
Preschool — Grade 1
(*Skills Focus: letter sound recognition, letter formation, squence writing, manuscript and dotted letter formats, skills achievement awards*)

by Marilynn G. Barr

Published by: Little Acorn Books™
Originally published by: Monday Morning Books, Inc.

Entire contents copyright © 2014 Little Acorn Books™

Little Acorn Books
PO Box 8787
Greensboro, NC 27419-0787

Promoting Early Skills for a Lifetime™

Little Acorn Books™
is an imprint of Little Acorn Associates, Inc.

http://www.littleacornbooks.com

Permission is hereby granted to reproduce student materials in this book for non-commercial individual or classroom use. *School-wide or system-wide use is expressly prohibited.

ISBN 978-1-937257-51-4
Printed in the United States of America

About Early Writing

Contents

Introduction 4
Writing Practice Boards
Writing Practice For Letter Aa 6
Writing Practice For Letter Bb 7
Writing Practice For Letter Cc 8
Writing Practice For Letter Dd 9
Writing Practice For Letter Ee................... 10
Writing Practice For Letter Ff 11
Writing Practice For Letter Gg................... 12
Writing Practice For Letter Hh................... 13
Writing Practice For Letter Ii..................... 14
Writing Practice For Letter Jj.................... 15
Writing Practice For Letter Kk................... 16
Writing Practice For Letter Ll 17
Writing Practice For Letter Mm................. 18
Writing Practice For Letter Nn.................. 19
Writing Practice For Letter Oo.................. 20
Writing Practice For Letter Pp 21
Writing Practice For Letter Qq.................. 22
Writing Practice For Letter Rr................... 23
Writing Practice For Letter Ss................... 24
Writing Practice For Letter Tt 25
Writing Practice For Letter Uu.................. 26
Writing Practice For Letter Vv 27
Writing Practice For Letter Ww................. 28
Writing Practice For Letter Xx 29
Writing Practice For Letter Yy 30
Writing Practice For Letter Zz................... 31
Writing Practice Cards 32
Uppercase Letters Writing Board 45
Lowercase Letters Writing Board 47
Number Writing Strips 49
Number Writing Board............................. 50
Trace-a-Letter Race 52
Game Boards... 53
Game Cards... 57
Awards Booklet 61
Awards 63
Take-Home Notes 64

About Early Writing

Introduction

Make letter writing practice fun with the ready-to-assemble patterns found in this book. *Early Writing* includes writing practice boards, cards, charts, a game, achievement awards, and take-home notes. Writing boards feature letter specific characters and objects with manuscript lines and dotted letters for each letter of the alphabet. Writing practice cards include two cards for each letter of the alphabet. These cards are designed to offer letter sound recognition as well as letter formation and sequence writing practice to form words. Writing practice charts provide individual letter formation practice. The Trace-a-Letter Race write-in game includes four game boards and alphabet picture cards for picture, sound, and letter recognition and writing practice. *Early Writing* is one of four titles in the "It's Fun to Learn™" series which includes: *Early Colors & Shapes, Early Math,* and *Early Reading."*

Writing Practice Boards
Provide plenty of writing practice with the boards on pages 6-31. Writing practice boards can be cut out or used as full page boards. Reproduce writing practice boards for children to color and cut out. Prepare a work station with crayons or markers for children to practice tracing letters. Mount finished boards on construction paper for display.

Form letter booklets when children have completed a board for each letter of the alphabet. Have children decorate construction paper covers. Then help each child stack and staple completed writing practice boards in alphabetical order.

Make reusable writing practice boards to include in a skills practice center. Color, cut out, and glue boards on construction paper. Laminate each board. Provide wipe-off crayons or markers and wiping cloth for children to practice tracing and erasing the boards.

Writing Practice Cards
Reproduce writing practice cards (pages 32-44) for more letter writing practice.

Reproduce, color, laminate, and cut out a set of cards. Place the cards with a wipe-off crayon or marker0 and wiping cloth in a basket. Place the basket in a writing skills practice center.

Reproduce cards for children to color, cut out, and trace the words. Have children glue each set of cards on a half sheet of construction paper for display.

Have children color, cut out, and glue a set of cards on a manila envelope. Have children cut out matching letter sound pictures from old magazines to place in envelopes. Invite each child to share his or her pictures during show and tell.

Trace-a-Letter Race
Children practice recognizing pictures, beginning letter sounds, and tracing letters as they play Trace-a-Letter Race (pages 52-60).

To play, each player chooses one of the four game boards. One player shuffles and places the tire game cards, face down, on the table. Each player, in turn, draws a card, names the picture on the card, identifies the beginning sound letter, then finds and traces the matching letter on his or her board. If there is no match, the player places the card, face down, in a discard pile, and the next player takes a turn. Play continues until each player has traced every letter on his or her game board. Reshuffle cards to continue play, if needed.

Awards
Children love to receive awards and keep track of their own achievements. Reproduce awards booklets (pages 61-62) for children to color and cut out. Help each child assemble and staple his or her booklet. Store all flower stickers in a basket. Give children flower stickers to glue in booklets as they master each listed skill.

Be prepared to reward children for writing skills achievement. Reproduce, color, and cut out a supply of awards (page 63) and store in a decorated awards envelope.

Take-Home Notes
Send home notes to keep parents informed about current writing skills practice. Reproduce and cut apart a supply of bright-colored paper notes (page 64). Store notes in a decorated manila envelope or folder.

Writing Practice For Letter Aa

Name ______________________ Date ______________________

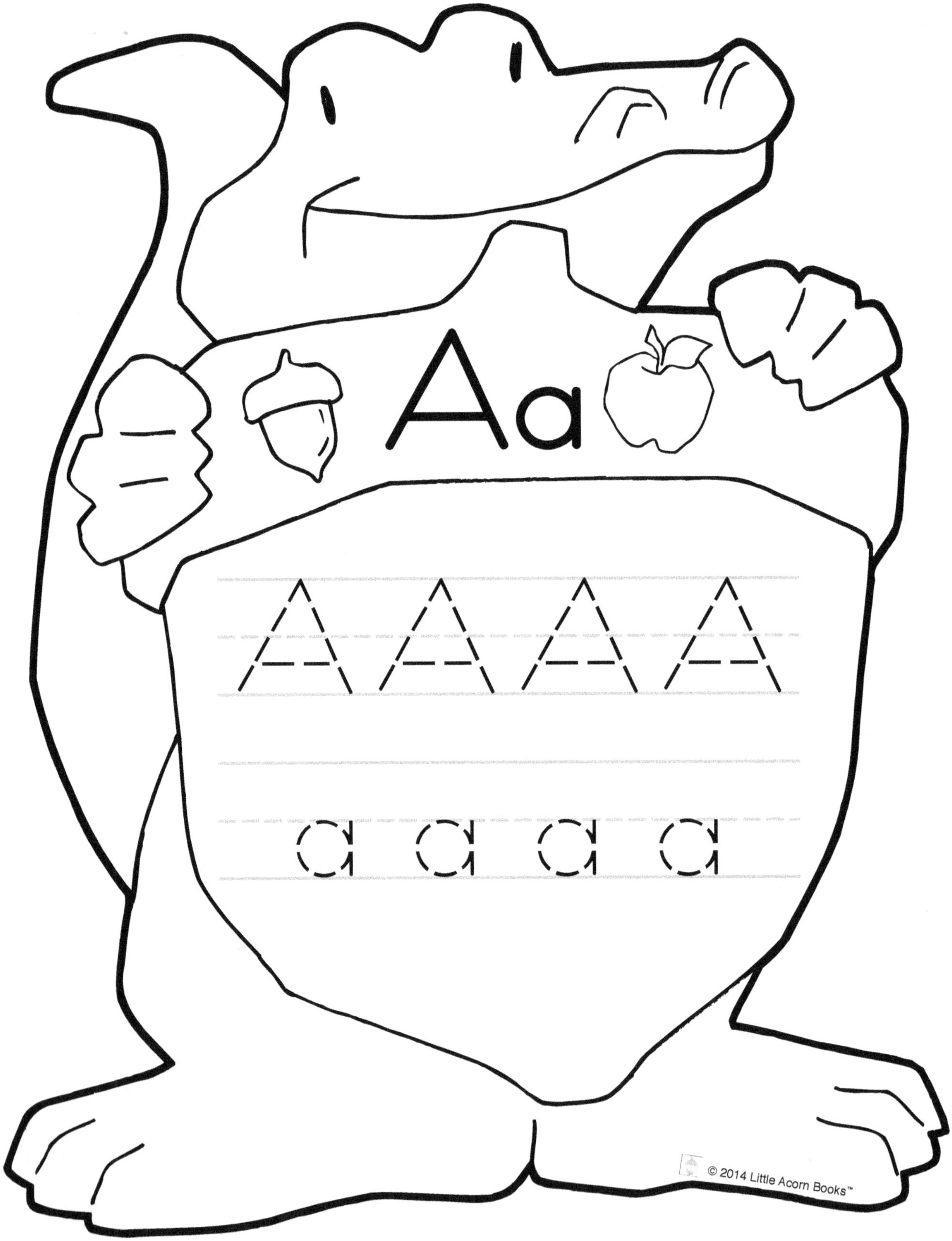

LAB20148P • About Early Writing • 978-1-937257-51-4 • © 2014 Little Acorn Books™

Writing Practice For Letter Bb

Name _____ Date _____

Writing Practice For Letter Cc

Name _____ Date _____

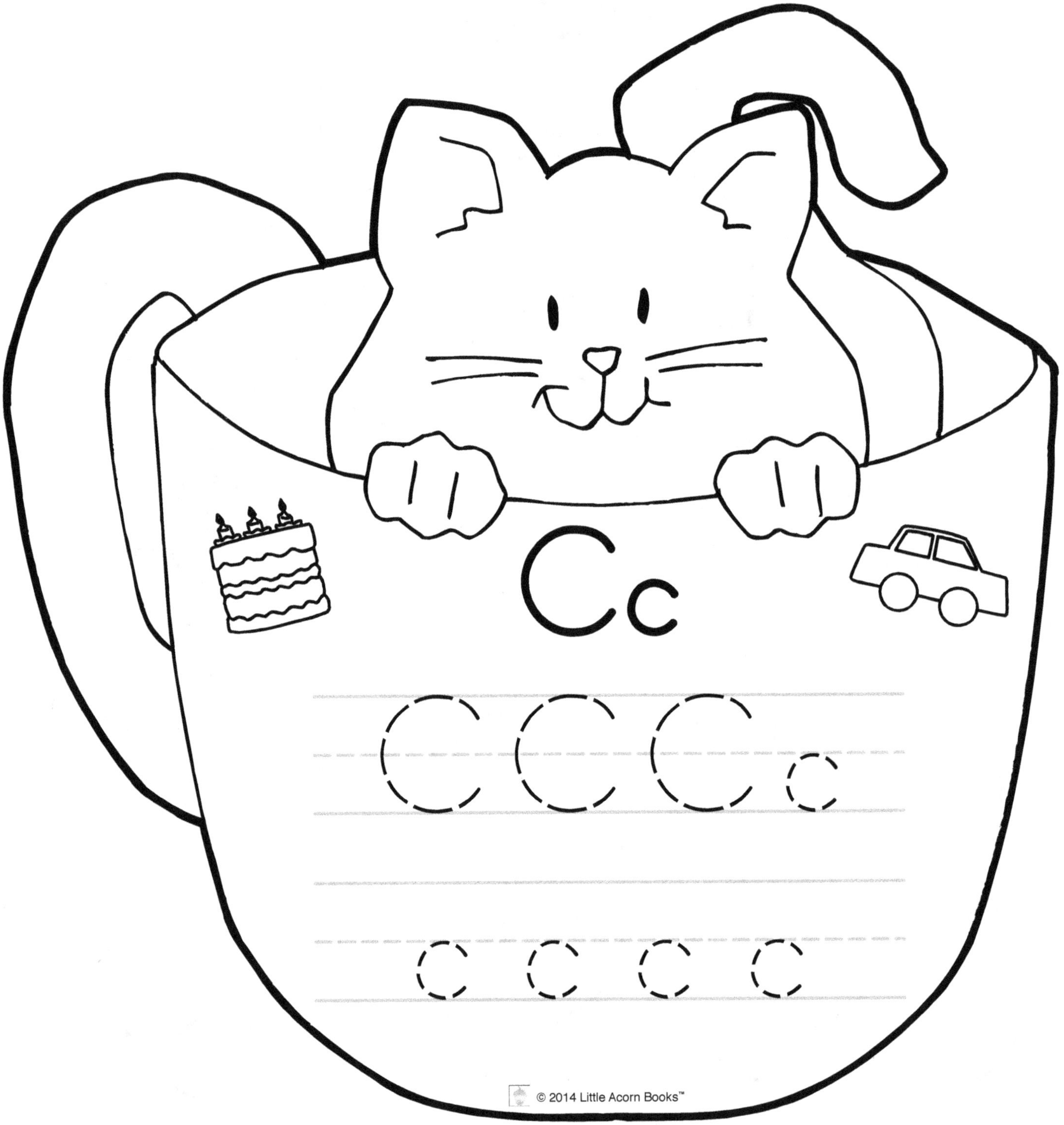

Writing Practice For Letter Dd

Name ______________________________ Date ____________________

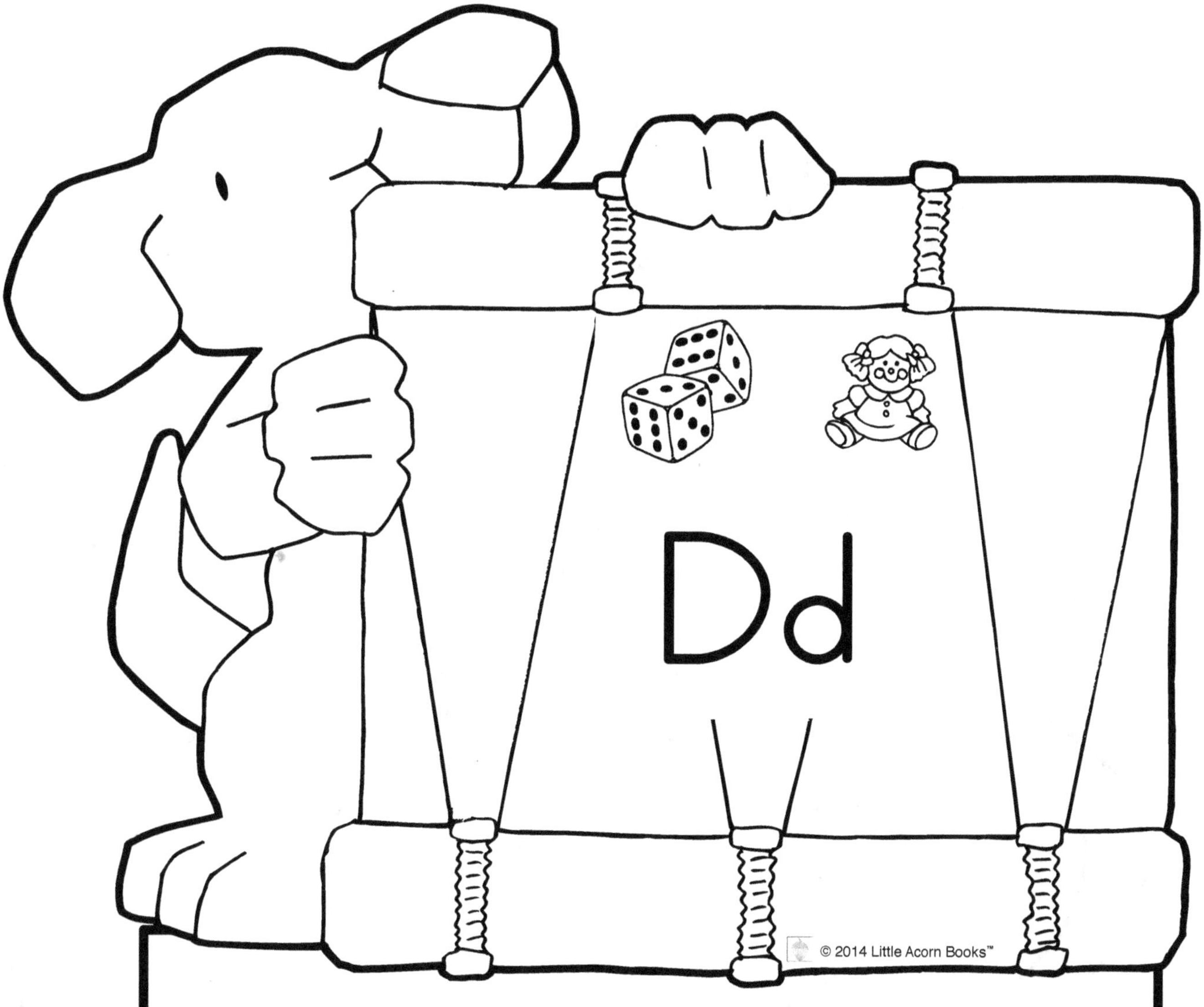

D D D D

d d d d

Writing Practice For Letter Ee

Name _____ Date _____

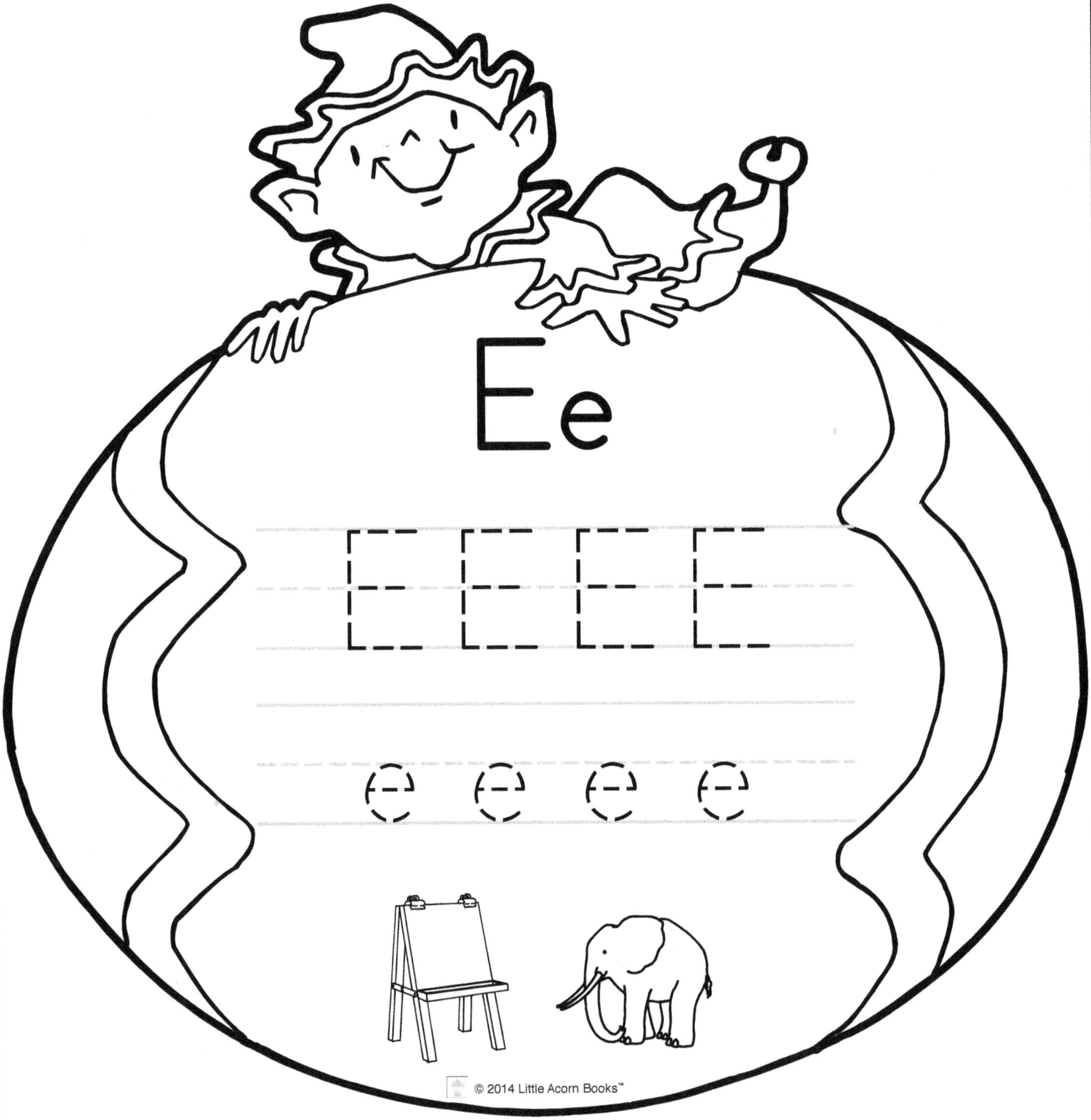

Ee

E E E E

e e e e

© 2014 Little Acorn Books™

Writing Practice For Letter Ff

Name _____   Date _____

Ff

F F F F

f f f f f

Writing Practice For Letter Gg

Name _____ Date _____

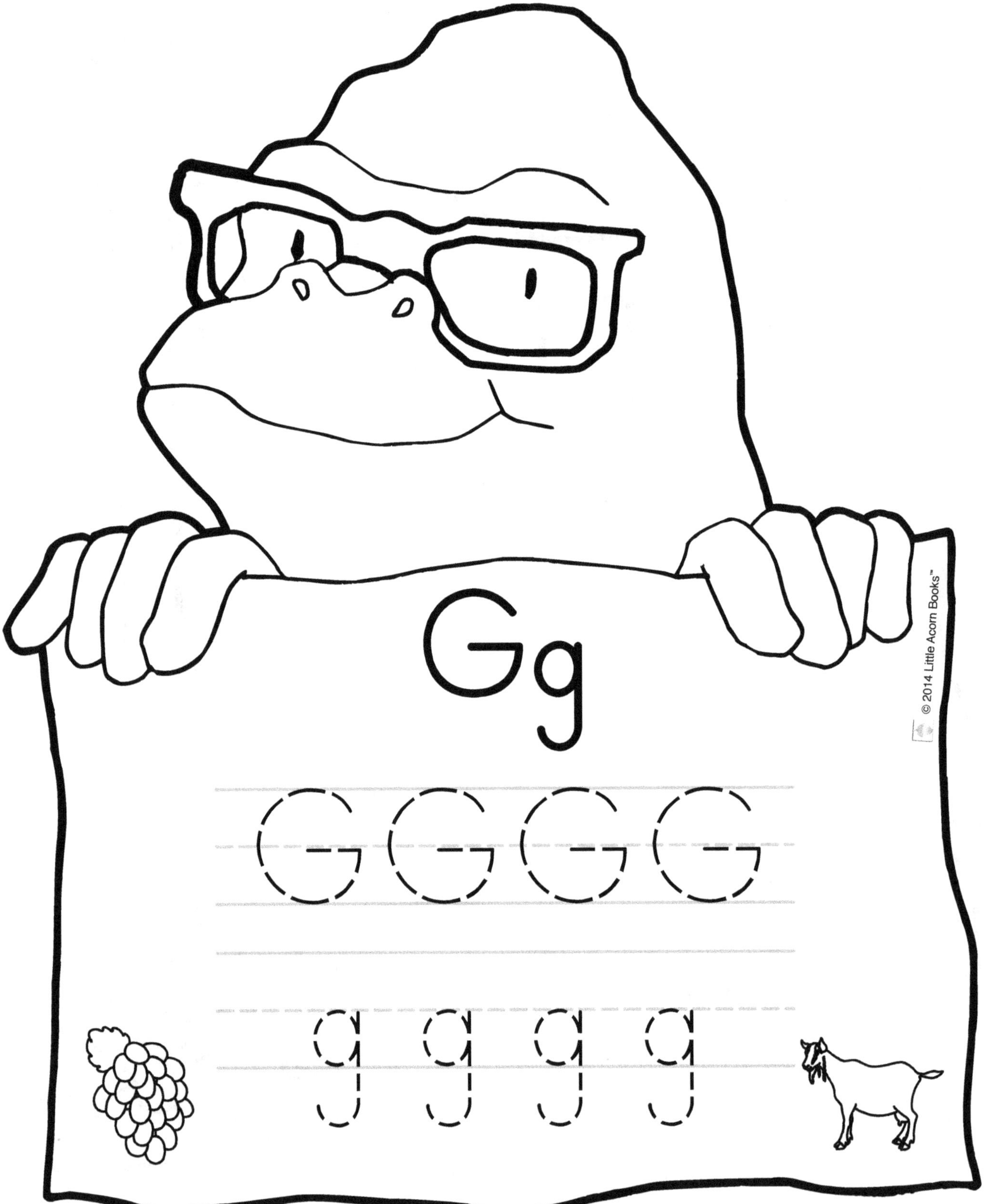

Gg

G G G G

g g g g

Writing Practice For Letter Hh

Name _____   Date _____

Hh

Writing Practice For Letter Ii

Name _____ Date _____

Indri

I i

Writing Practice For Letter Jj

Name _____ Date _____

Writing Practice For Letter Kk

Name _____ Date _____

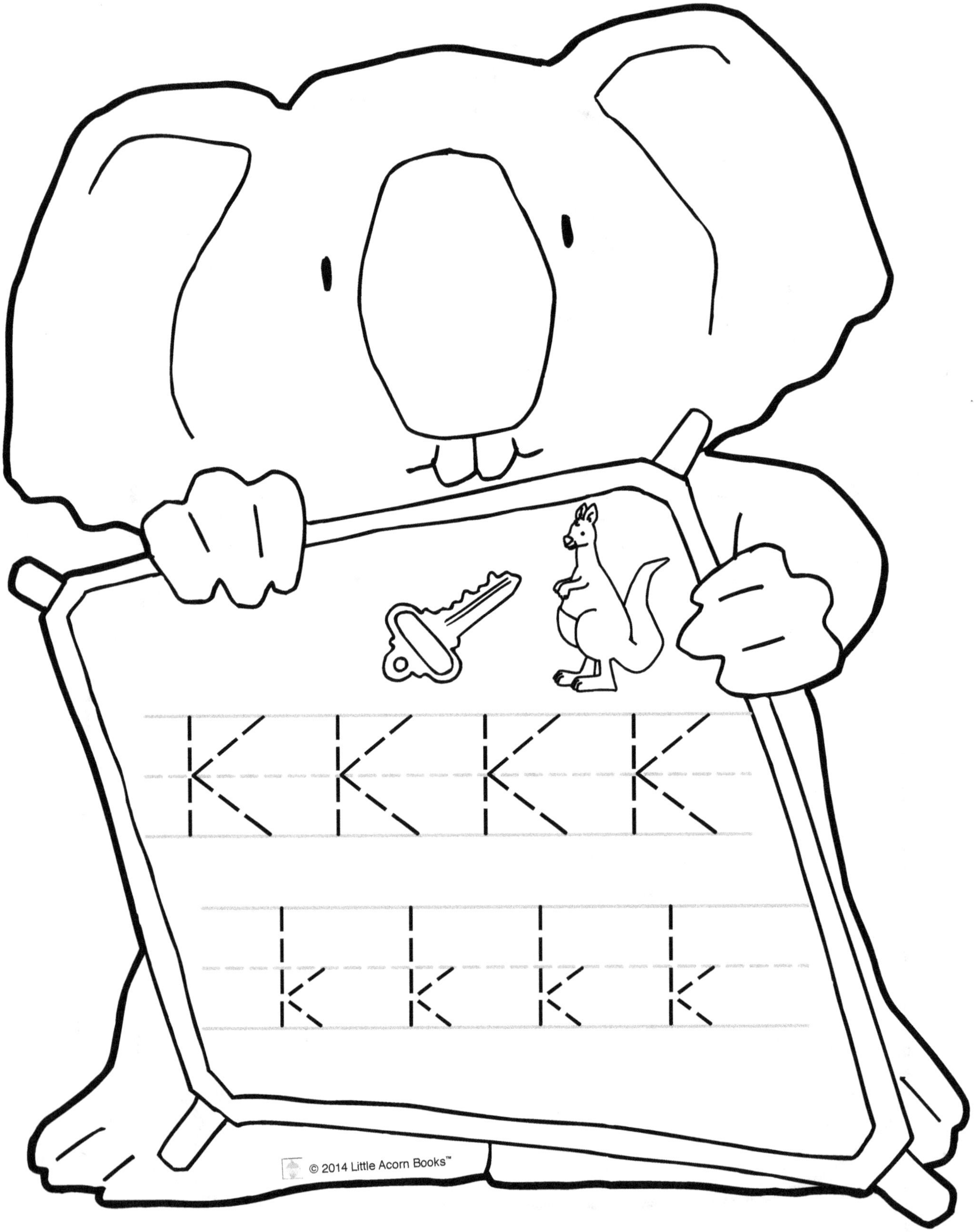

Writing Practice For Letter Ll

Name _____ Date _____

Writing Practice For Letter Mm

Name _____ Date _____

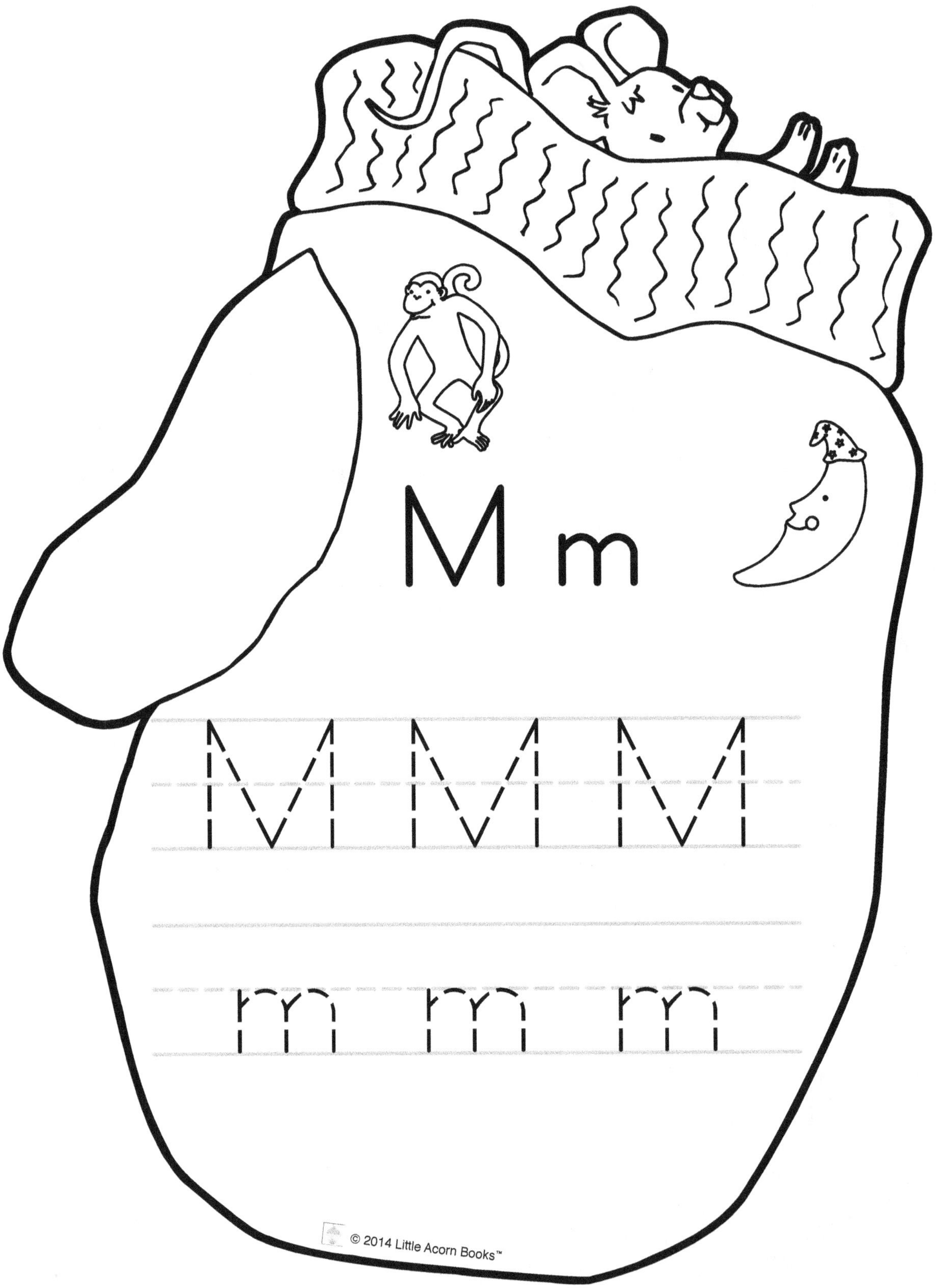

Writing Practice For Letter Nn

Name _____ Date _____

The News

Giant Narwhal Discovered

N n

N N N N N

n n n n n

Writing Practice For Letter Oo

Name _____ Date _____

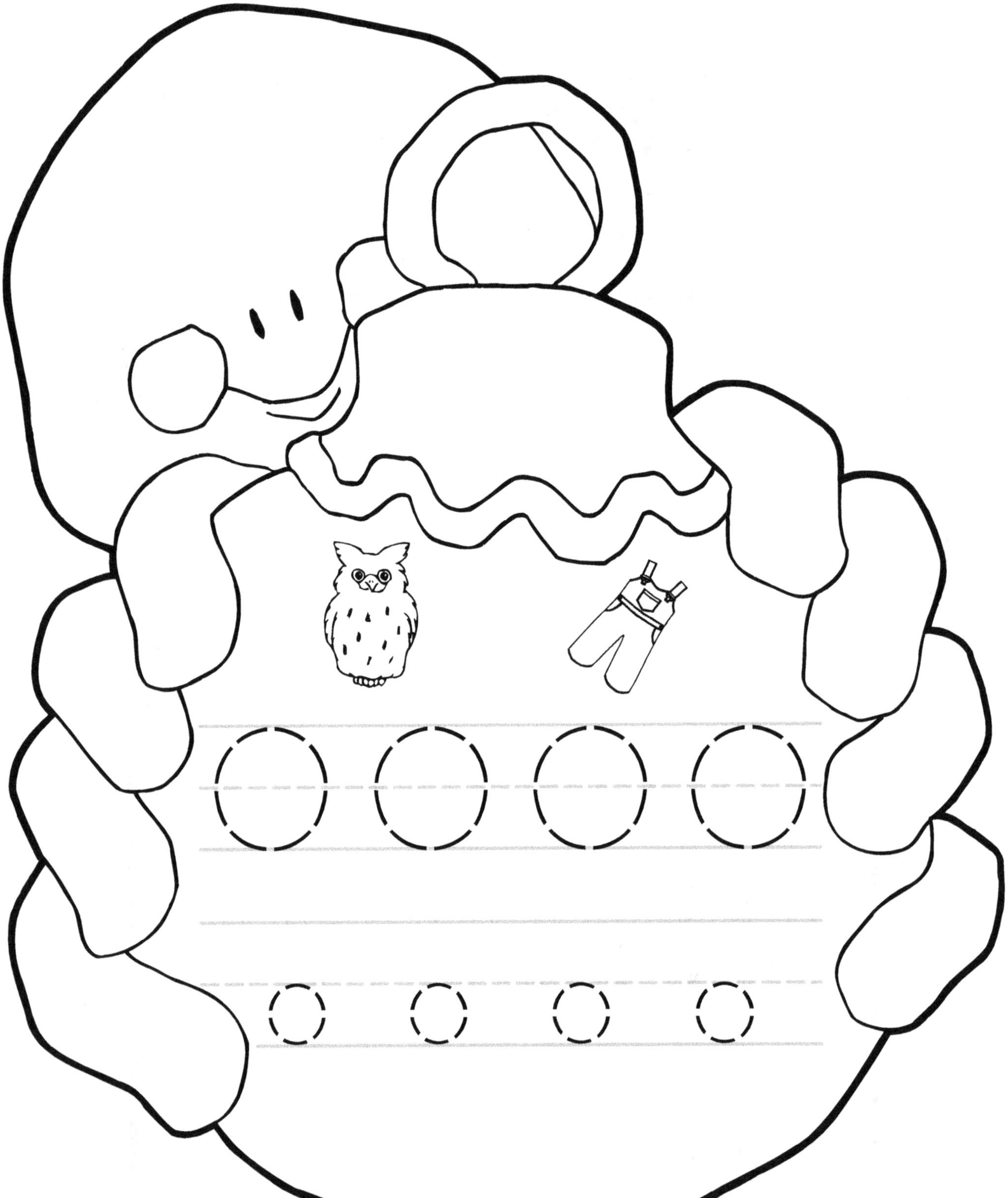

Writing Practice For Letter Pp

Name _____ Date _____

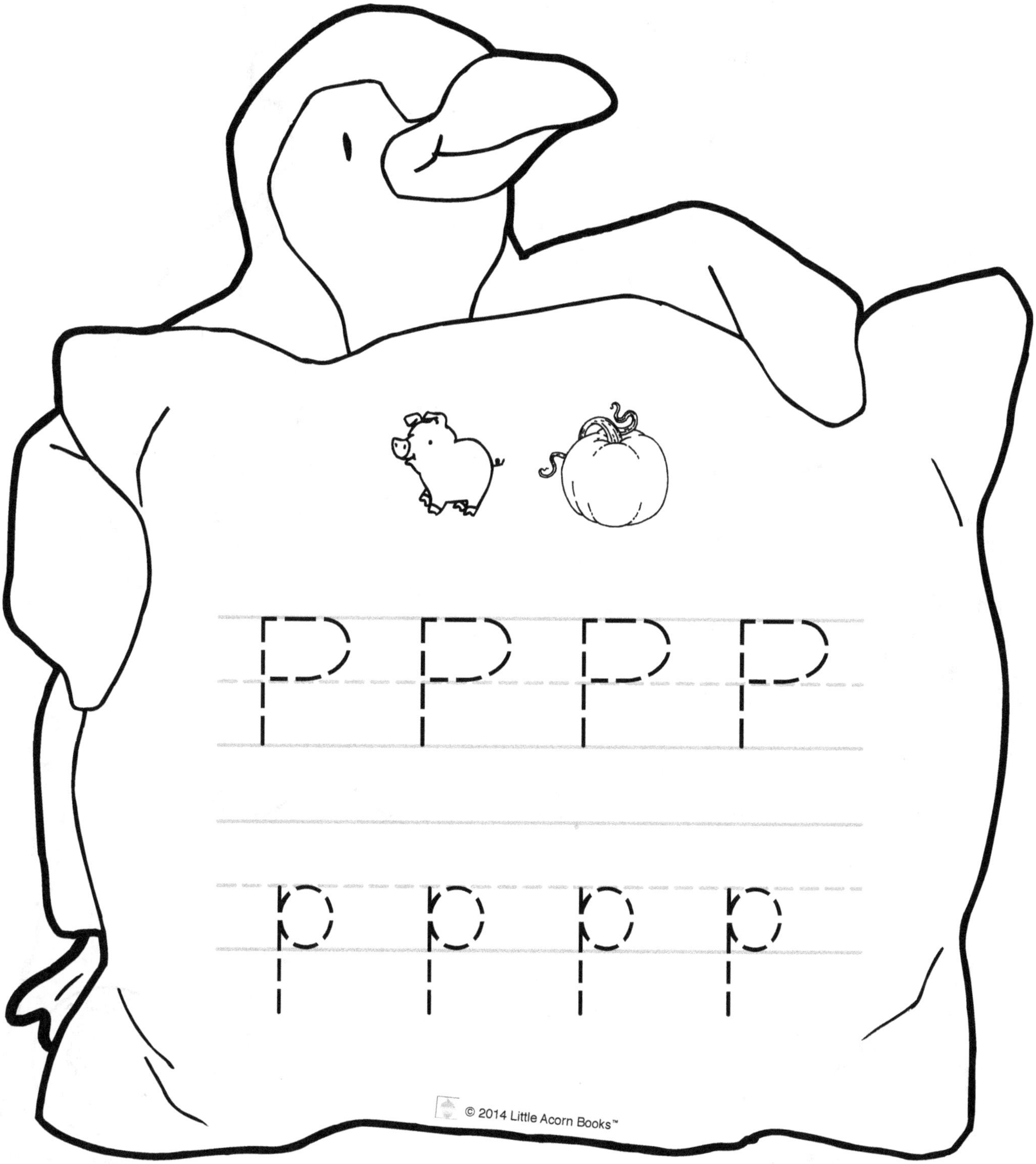

P P P P

p p p p

LAB20148P • About Early Writing • 978-1-937257-51-4 • © 2014 Little Acorn Books™

Writing Practice For Letter Qq

Name _____ Date _____

Writing Practice For Letter Rr

Name _____ Date _____

R R R

r r r

Writing Practice For Letter Ss

Name ______________________ Date ______________

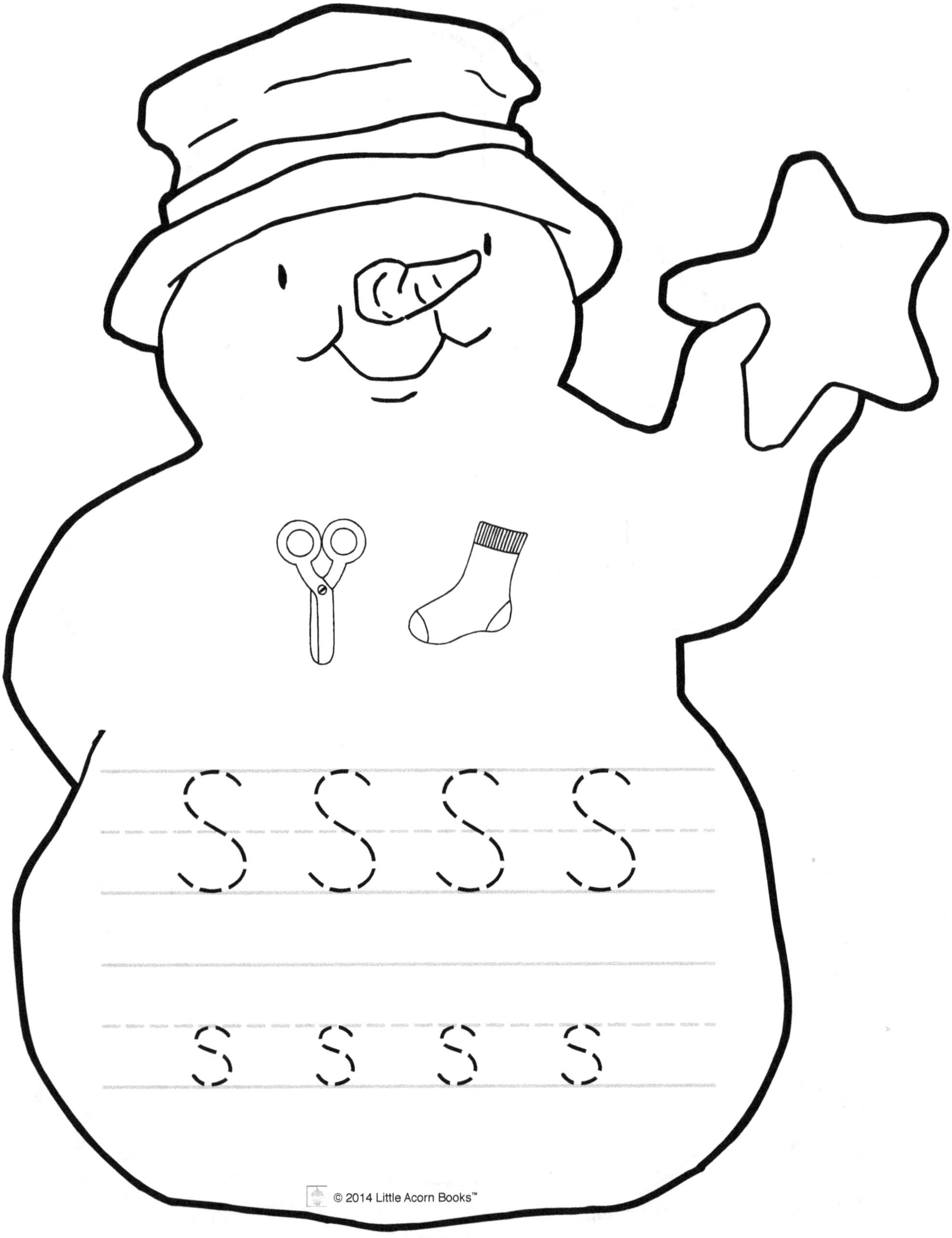

LAB20148P • About Early Writing • 978-1-937257-51-4 • © 2014 Little Acorn Books™

Writing Practice For Letter Tt

Name _____ Date _____

Writing Practice For Letter Uu

Name _____ Date _____

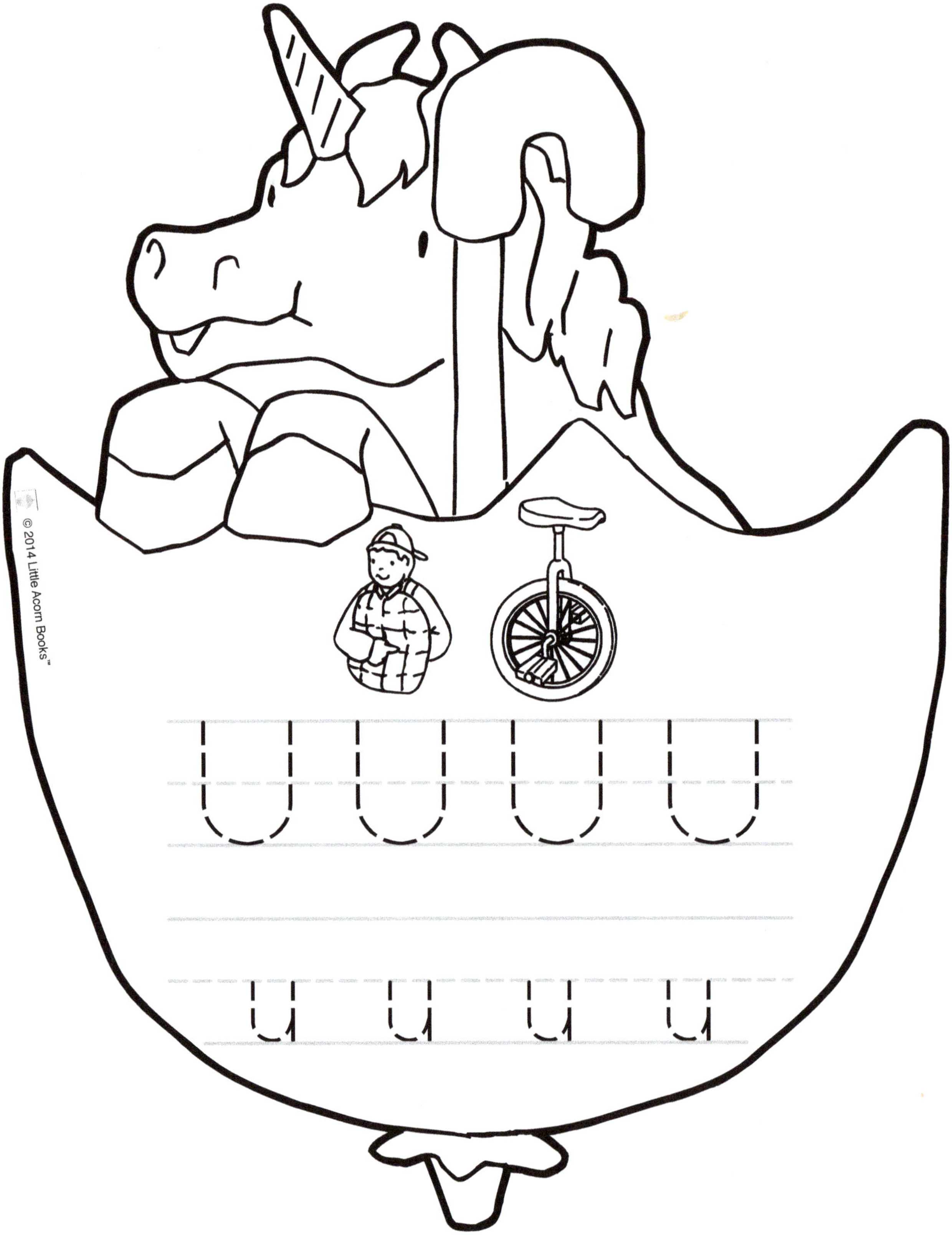

Writing Practice For Letter Vv

Name _____ Date _____

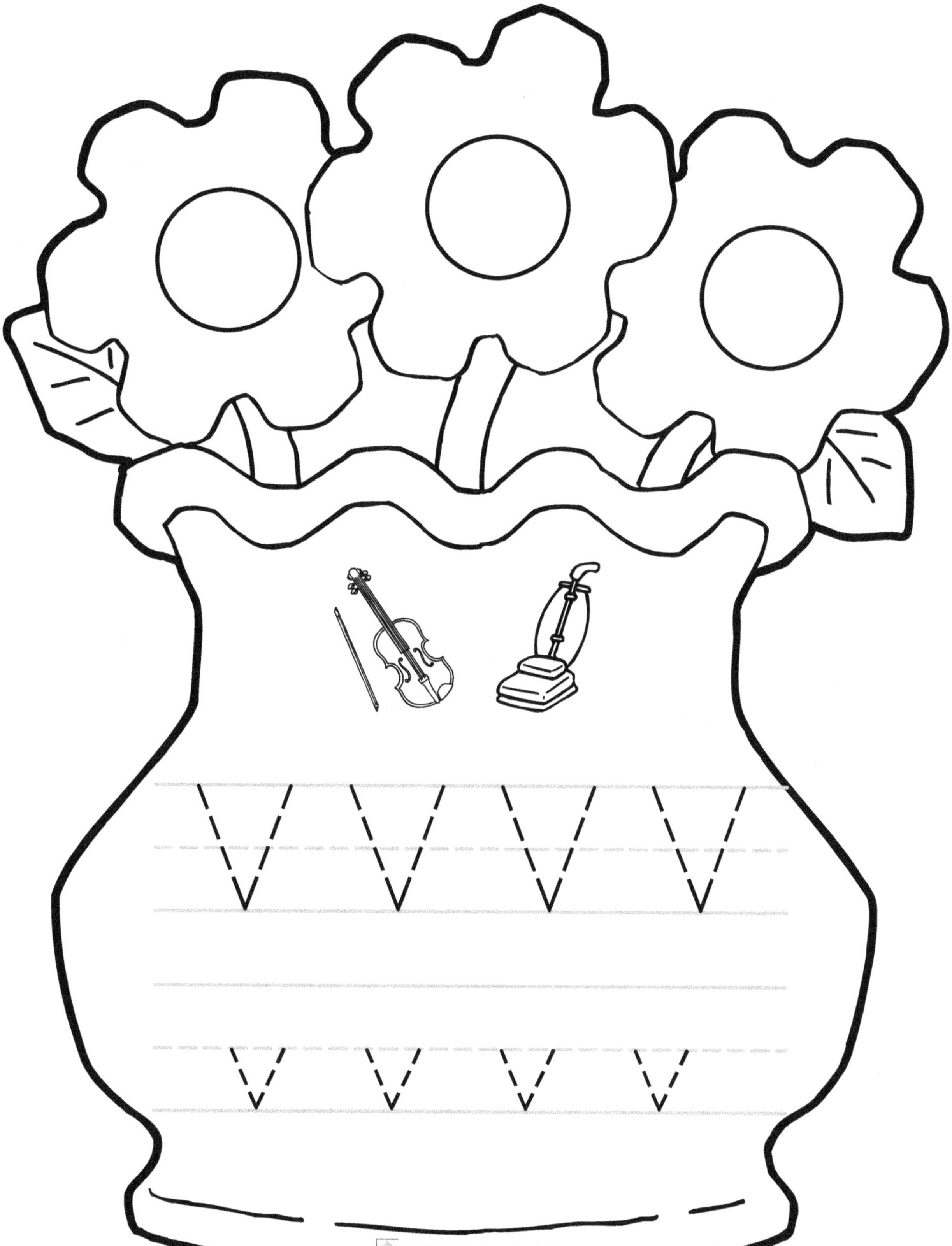

Writing Practice For Letter Ww

Name _____ Date _____

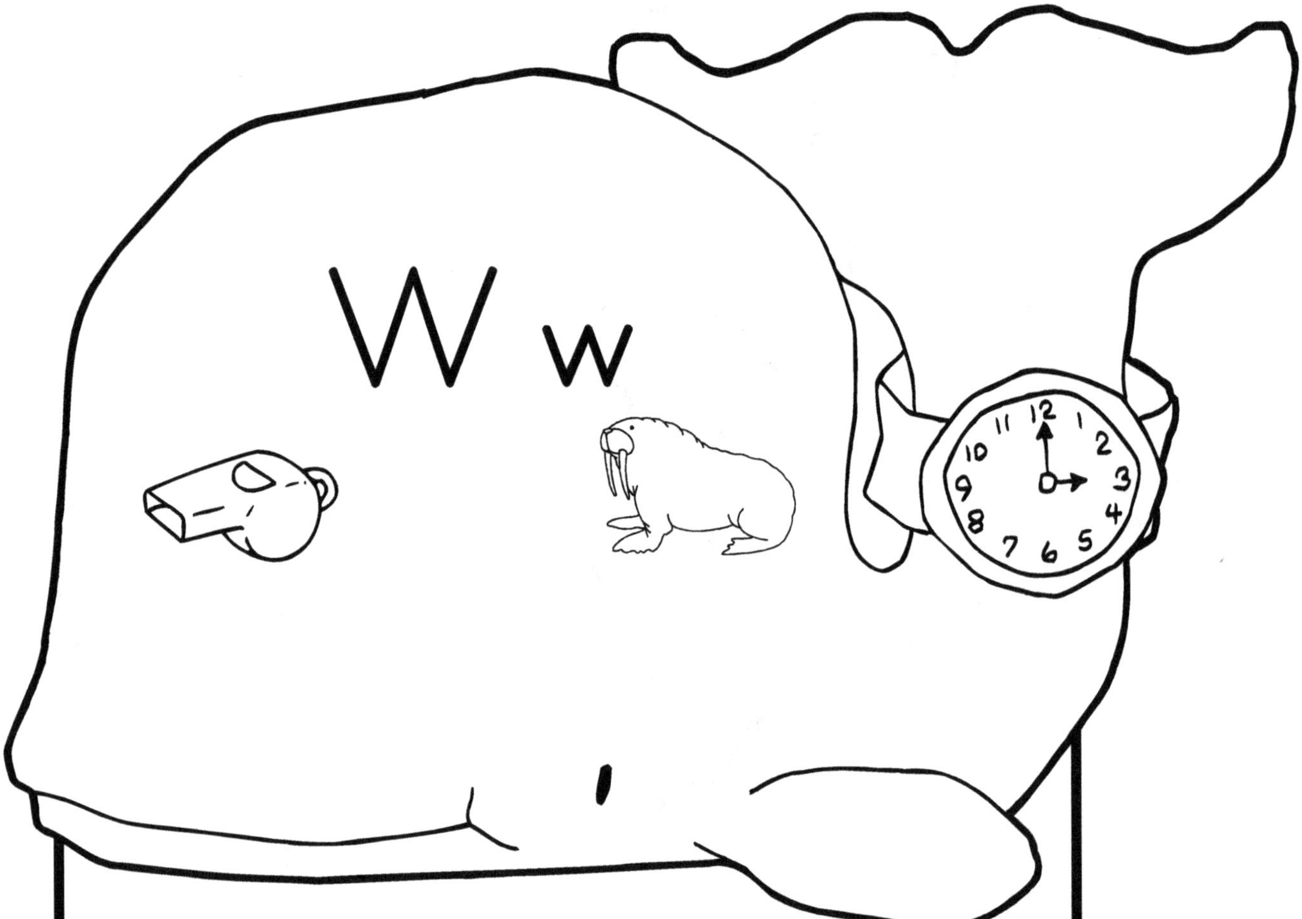

Writing Practice For Letter Xx

Name _____ Date _____

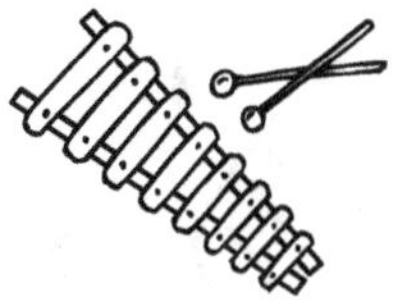

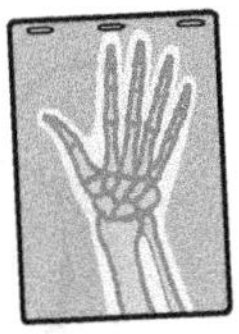

Writing Practice For Letter Yy

Name ______________________ Date ______________________

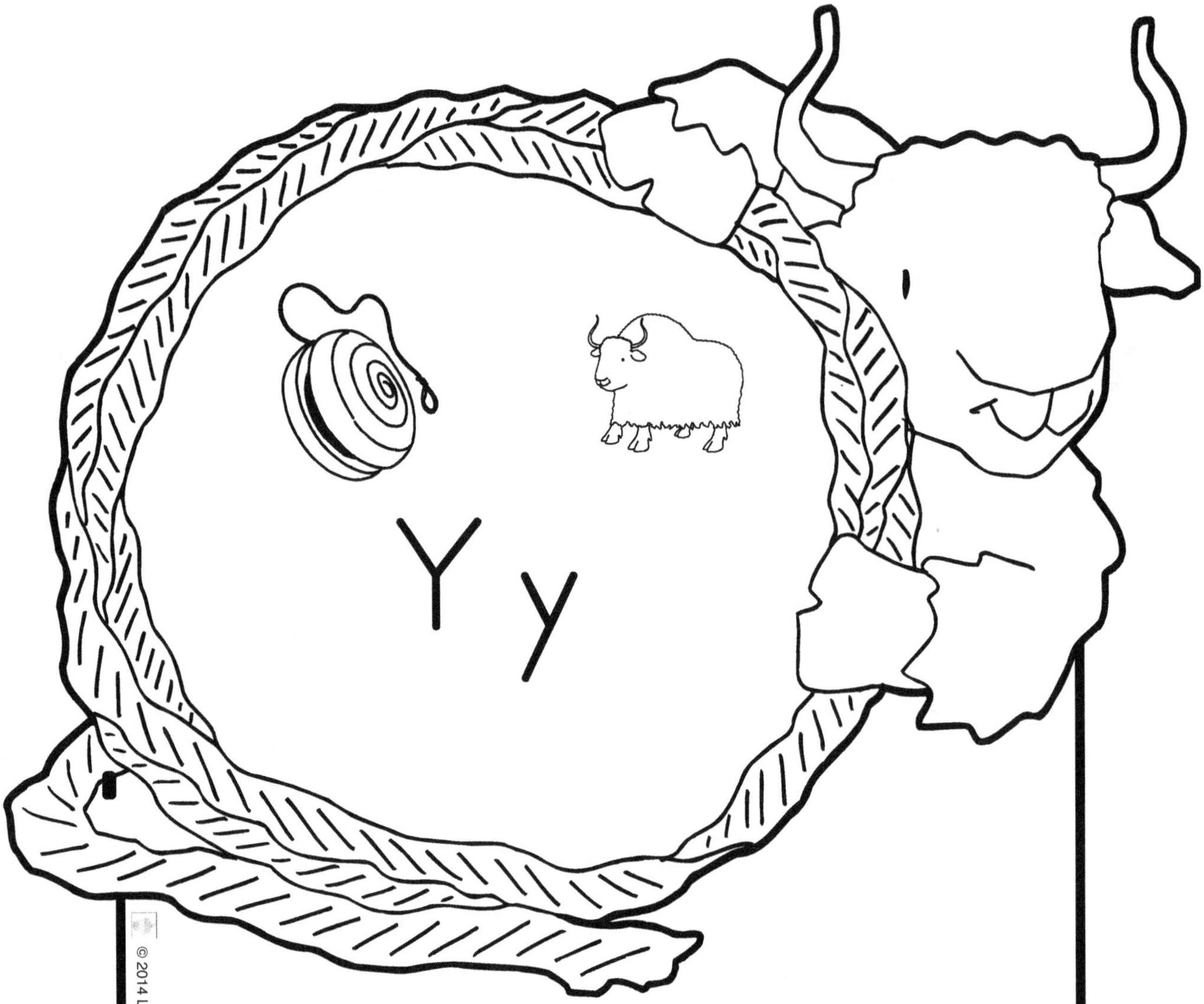

Y Y Y Y

y y y y

LAB20148P • About Early Writing • 978-1-937257-51-4 • © 2014 Little Acorn Books™

Writing Practice For Letter Zz

Name _____   Date _____

Z Z Z Z

Z Z Z Z

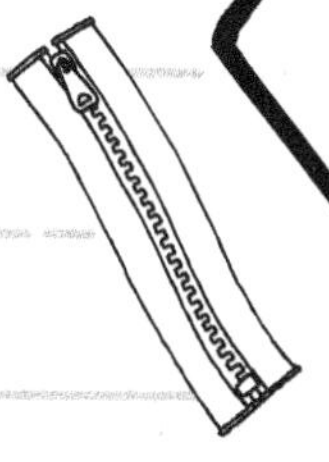

Writing Practice Cards

A B C D E F G H I J K L M

N O P Q R S T U V W X Y Z

Writing Practice Cards

A B C D E F G H I J K L M

N O P Q R S T U V W X Y Z

Writing Practice Cards

A B C D E F G H I J K L M

egg

easel

frog

fox

N O P Q R S T U V W X Y Z

Writing Practice Cards

A B C D E F G H I J K L M

N O P Q R S T U V W X Y Z

Writing Practice Cards

A B C D E F G H I J K L M

ice

igloo

jar

jack

N O P Q R S T U V W X Y Z

Writing Practice Cards

A B C D E F G H I J K L M

kite

key

lion

lamp

N O P Q R S T U V W X Y Z

Writing Practice Cards

A B C D E F G H I J K L M

N O P Q R S T U V W X Y Z

Writing Practice Cards

A B C D E F G H I J K L M

owl

overalls

pig

pan

N O P Q R S T U V W X Y Z

LAB20148P • About Early Writing • 978-1-937257-51-4 • © 2014 Little Acorn Books™   39

Writing Practice Cards

A B C D E F G H I J K L M

N O P Q R S T U V W X Y Z

Writing Practice Cards

A B C D E F G H I J K L M

N O P Q R S T U V W X Y Z

Writing Practice Cards

A B C D E F G H I J K L M

N O P Q R S T U V W X Y Z

Writing Practice Cards

A B C D E F G H I J K L M

N O P Q R S T U V W X Y Z

Writing Practice Cards

A B C D E F G H I J K L M

N O P Q R S T U V W X Y Z

Uppercase Letters Writing Board

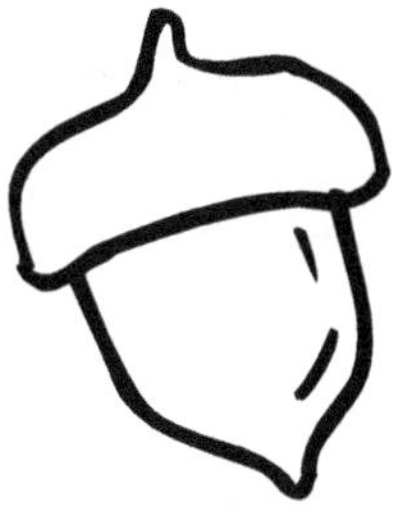		A	B
E	F	G	H
M	N	O	P
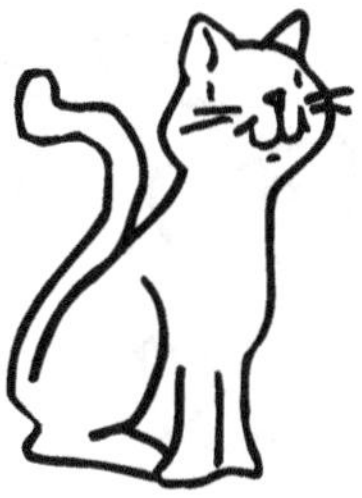	U	V	W

Uppercase Letters Writing Board

C	D	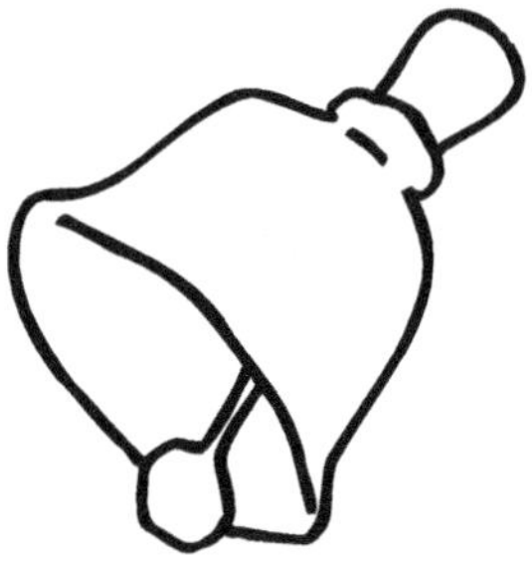	
I	J	K	L
Q	R	S	T
X	Y	Z	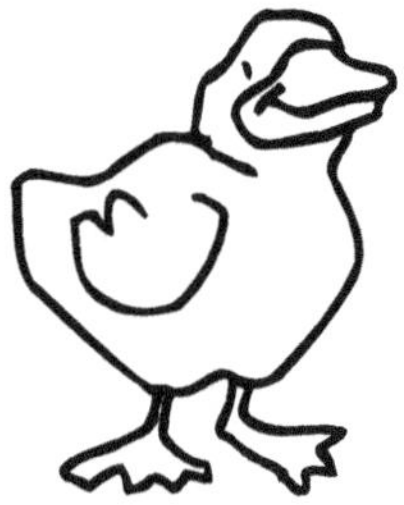

LAB20148P • About Early Writing • 978-1-937257-51-4 •

Lowercase Letters Writing Board

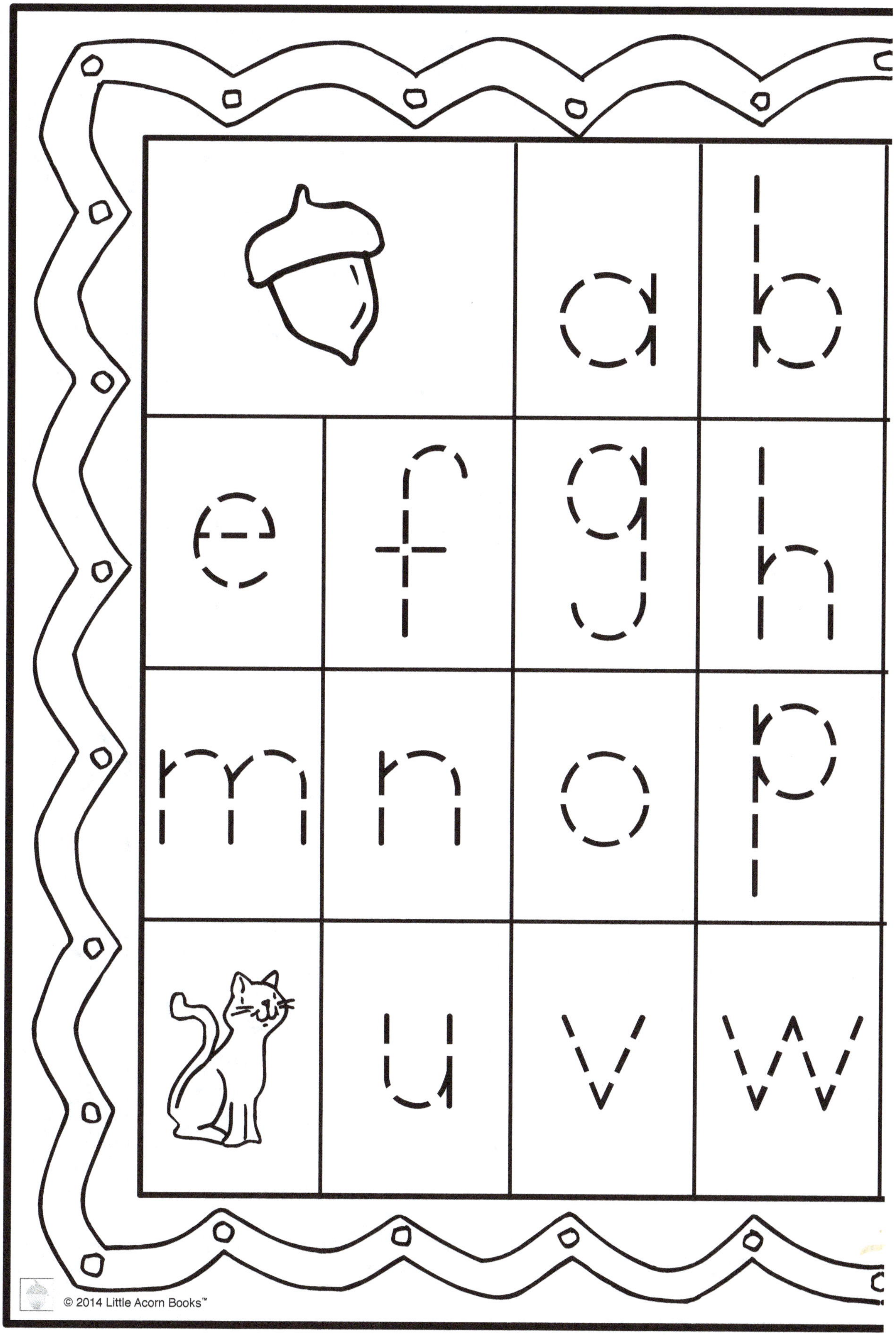

Lowercase Letters Writing Board

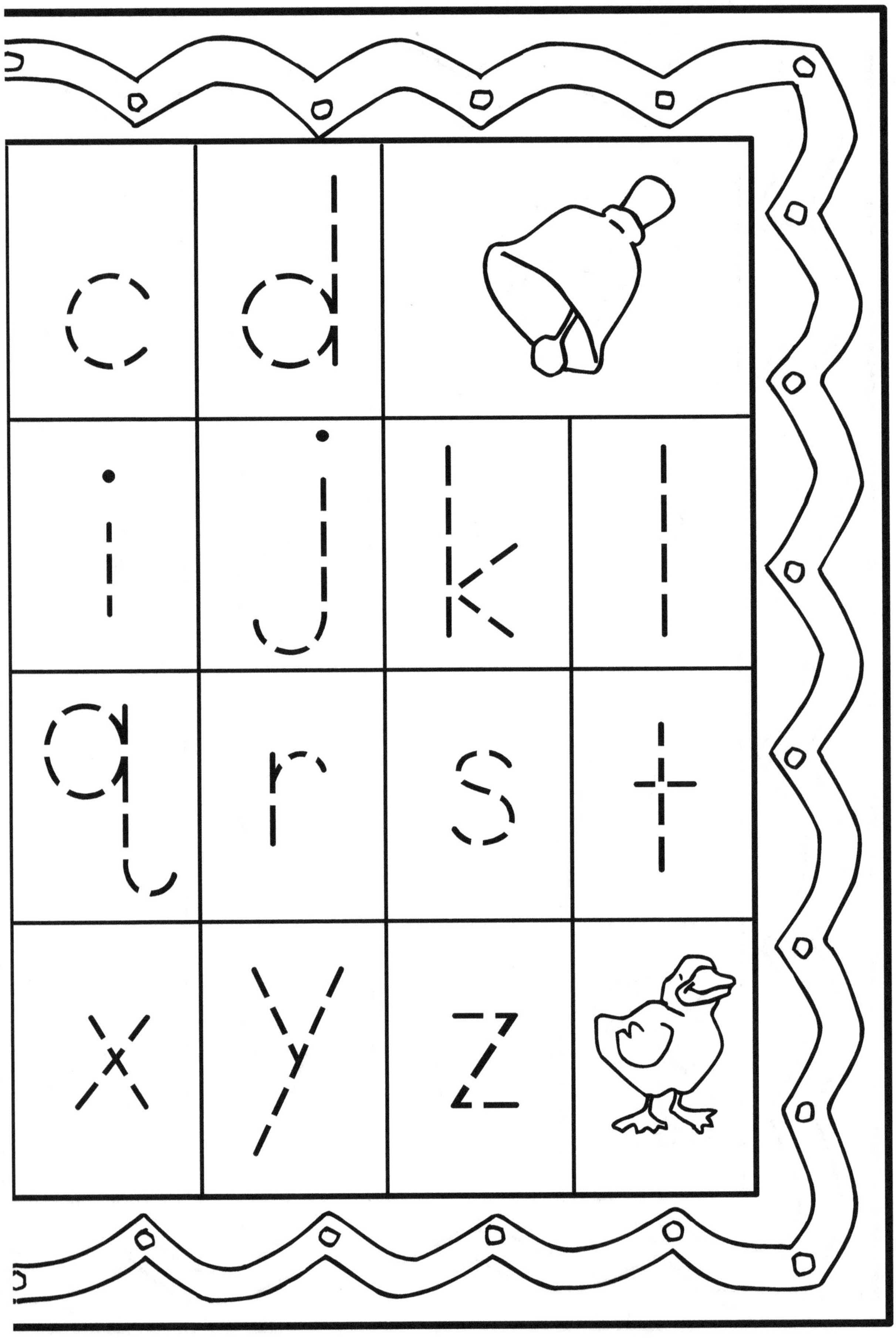

c d

i j k l

q r s t

x y z

Number Writing Strips

1 1	one one
2 2	two two
3 3	three three
4 4	four four
5 5	five five
6 6	six six
7 7	seven seven
8 8	eight eight
9 9	nine nine
10 10	ten ten

Reproduce, color, cut out, and laminate the Number Writing Board patterns (pages 50-51). Reproduce, laminate, and cut out a set of oak tag number writing strips.

Children trace the numerals and number words on each writing strip. Then they place each strip on the matching space on the Number Writing Board.

Provide a wipe-off crayon and wiping cloth to write and erase numerals or number words directly on the laminated writing board.

Number Writing Board

Number Writing Board

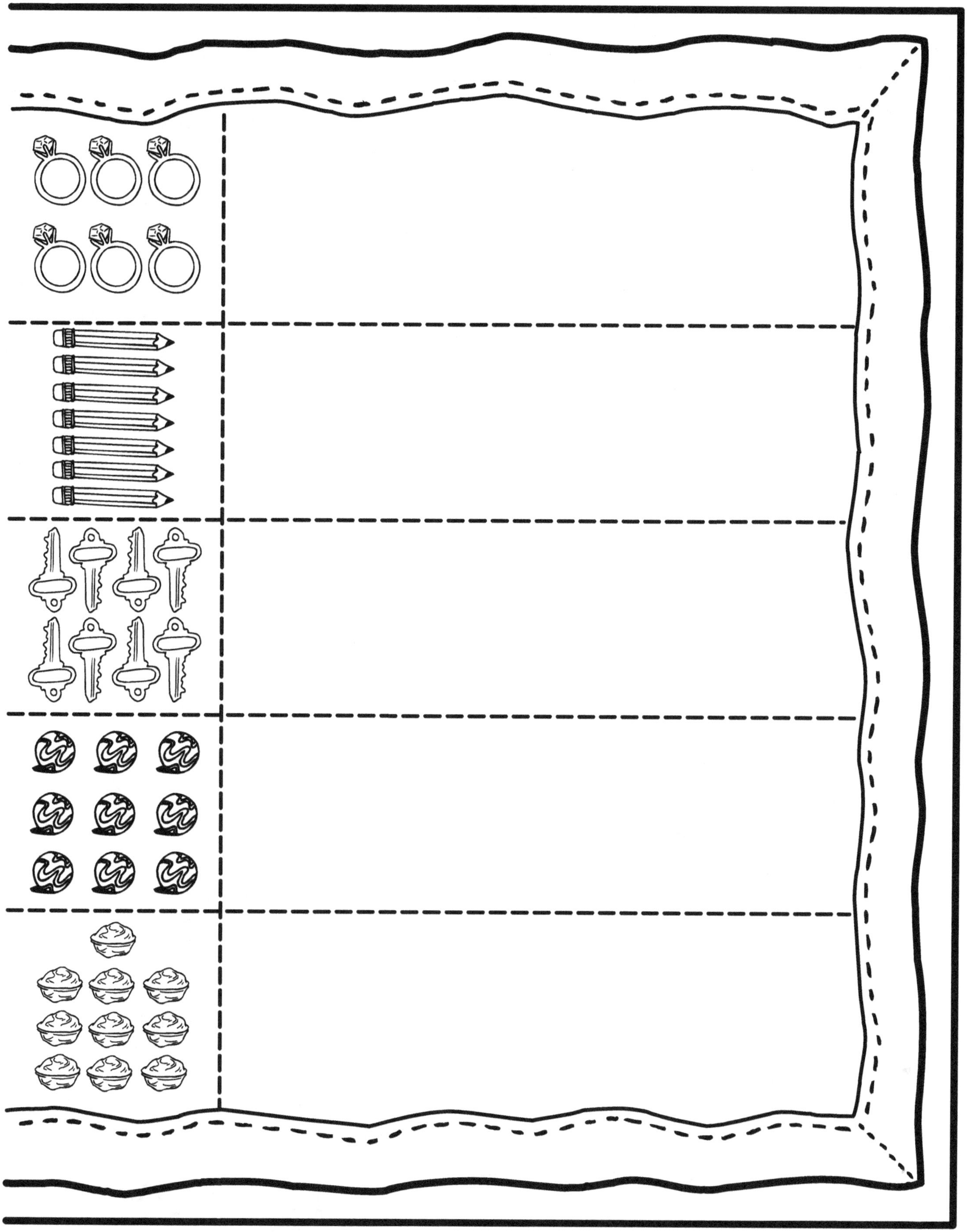

Trace-a-Letter Race

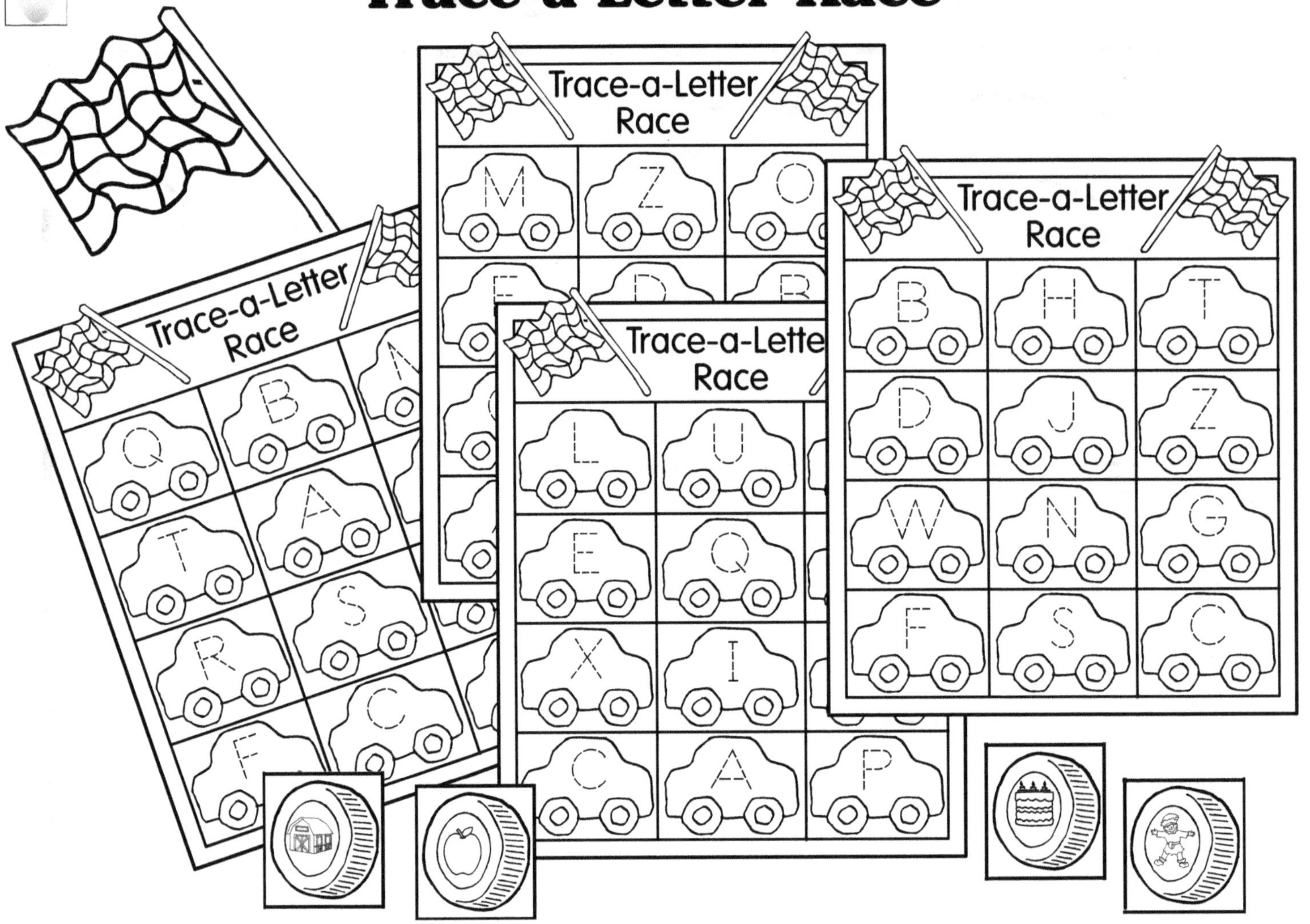

Reproduce, color, and cut out the game board patterns and game cards. Glue each game board pattern to a sheet of oak tag or construction paper. Laminate the game boards and game cards. Cut apart the game cards. Decorate a manila envelope to store the game boards and cards.

Option: Reproduce, color, and glue each page of game cards to the back of a sheet of gift wrap, then laminate and cut out the cards.

Trace-a-Letter Race Game Board

Trace-a-Letter Race

M	Z	O
F	D	B
G	V	K
A	R	Y

Trace-a-Letter Race Game Board

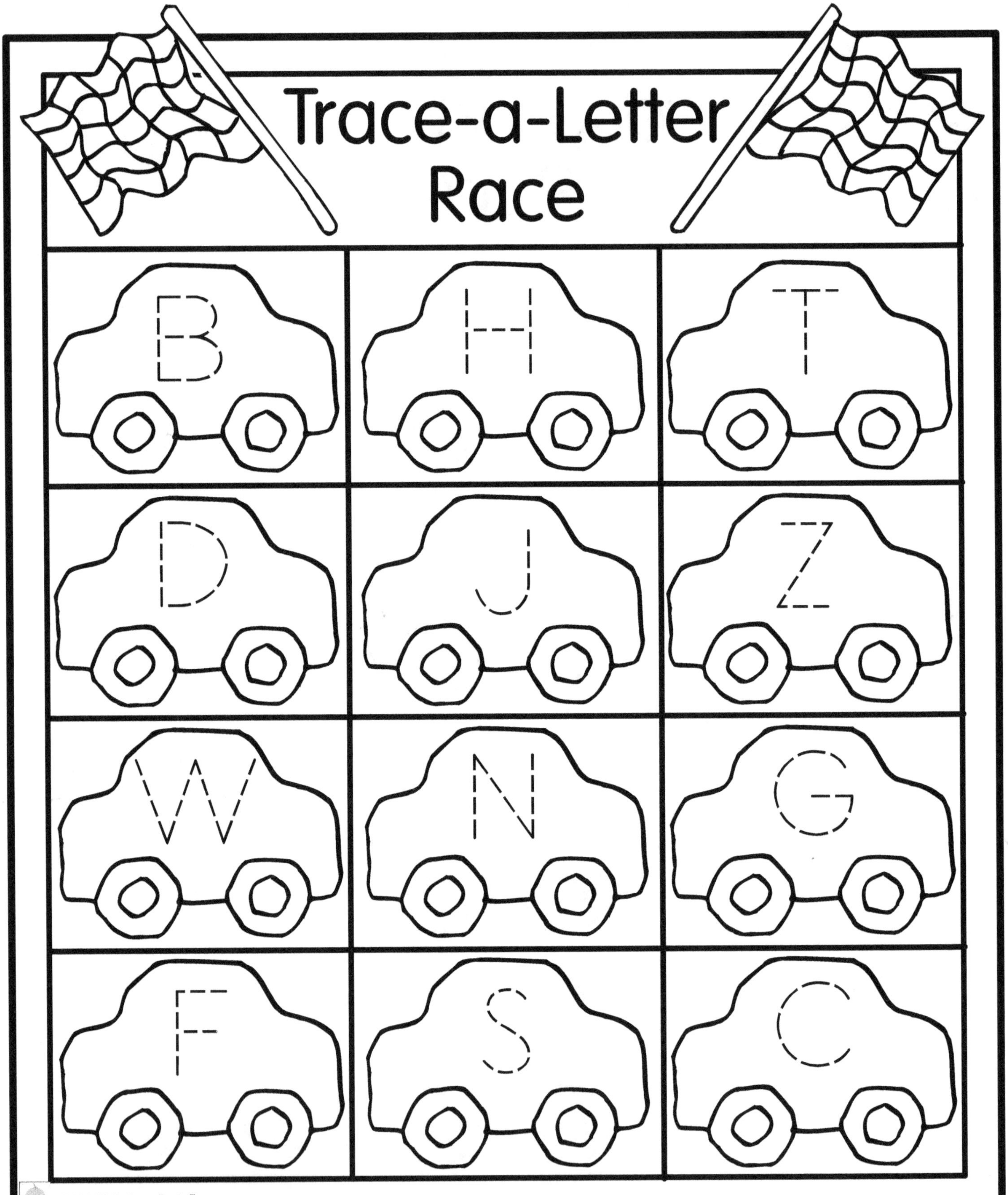

Trace-a-Letter Race

B	H	T
D	J	Z
W	N	G
F	S	C

Trace-a-Letter Race Game Board

Trace-a-Letter Race

L	U	E
E	Q	H
X	I	N
C	A	P

Trace-a-Letter Race Game Board

Trace-a-Letter Race Game Cards

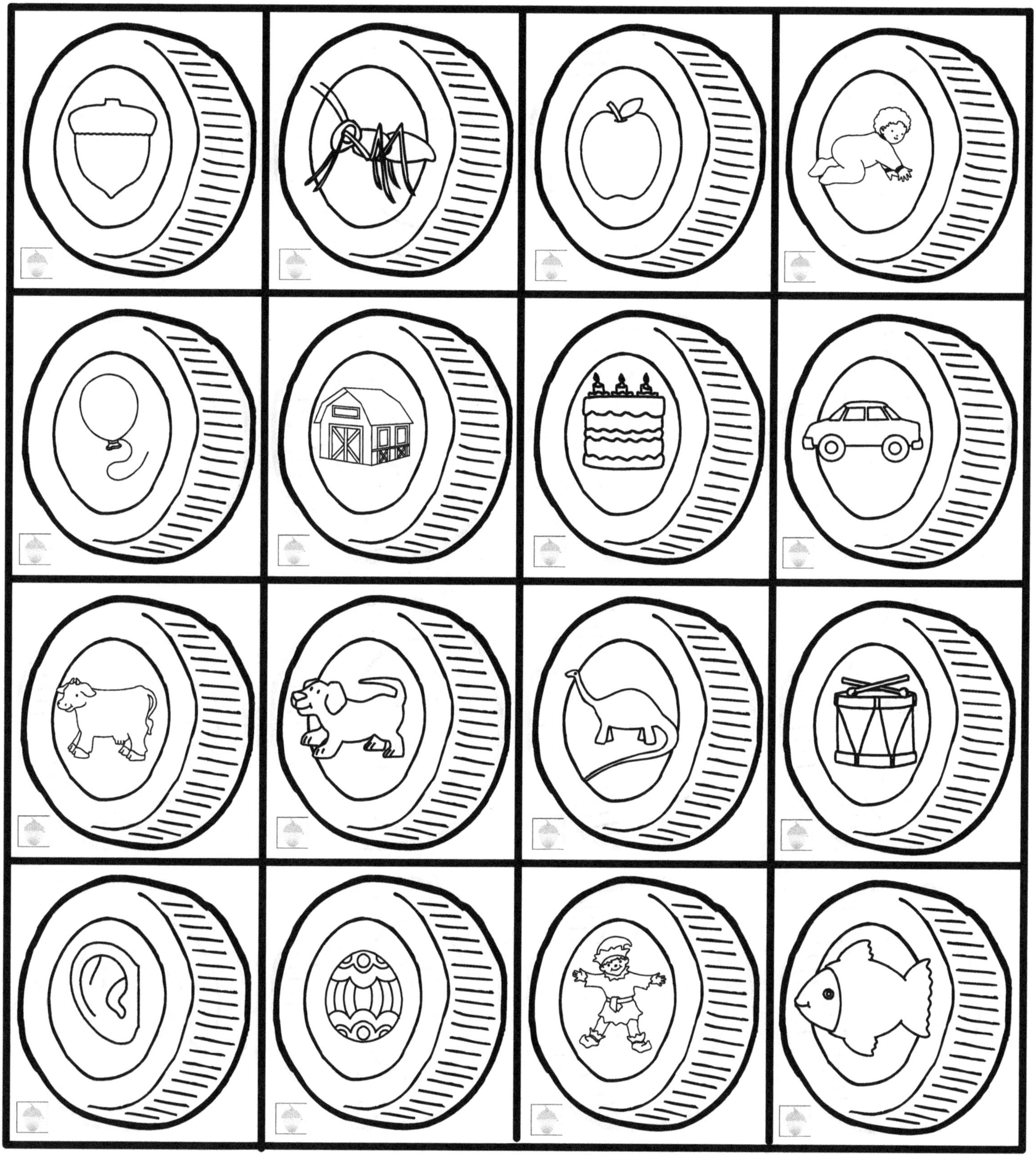

Trace-a-Letter Race Game Cards

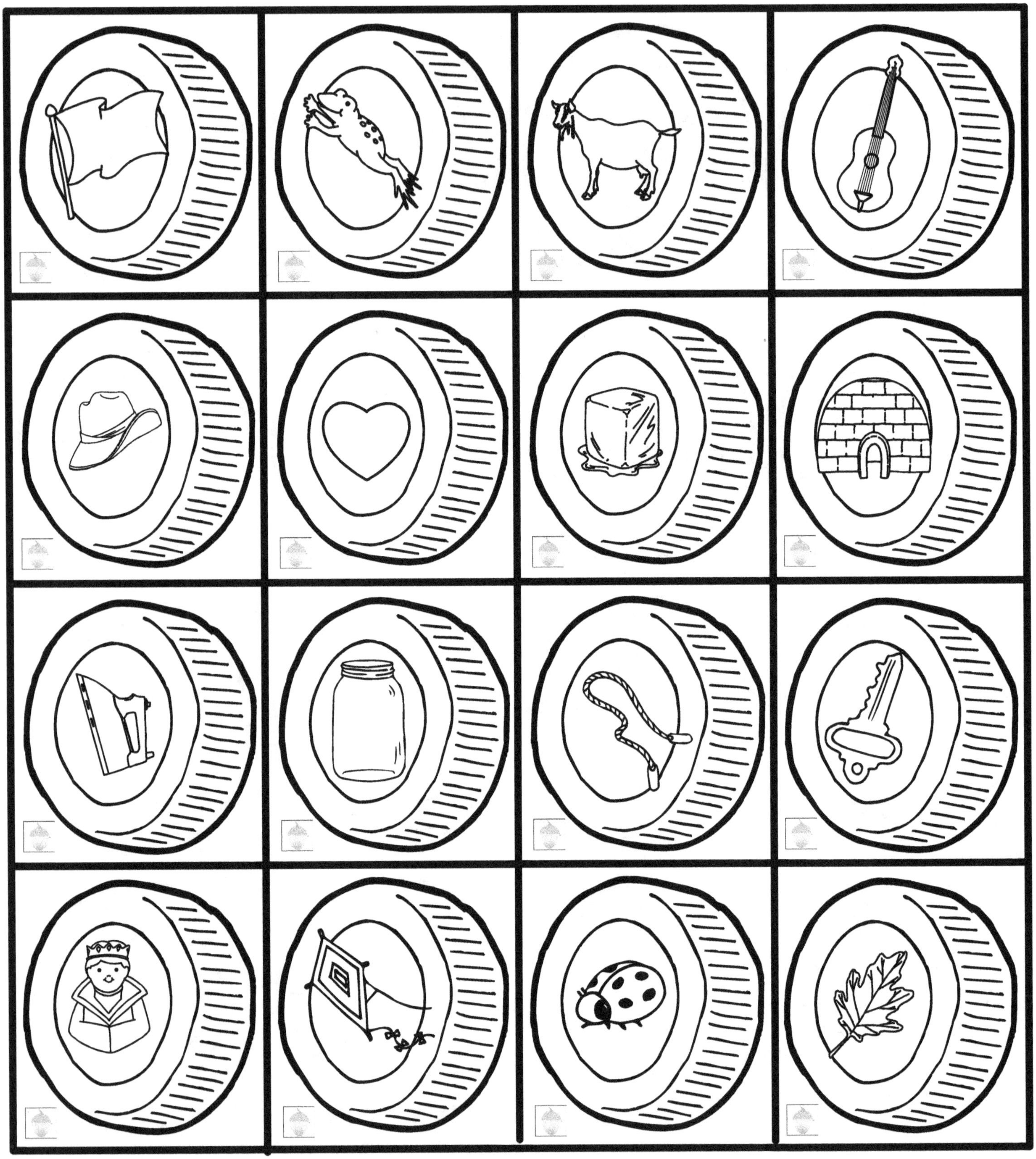

Trace-a-Letter Race Game Cards

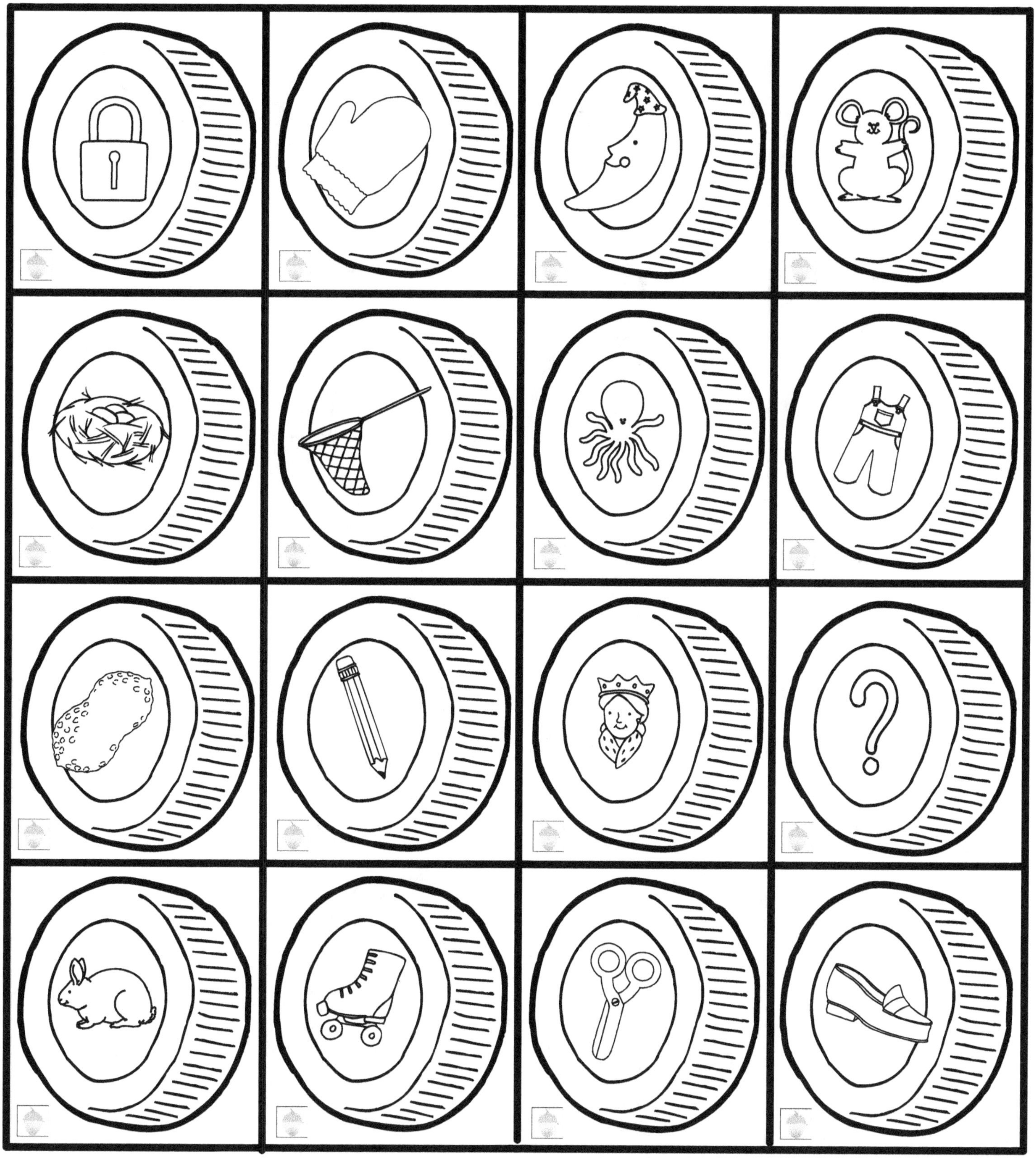

LAB20148P • About Early Writing • 978-1-937257-51-4 • © 2014 Little Acorn Books™ 59

Trace-a-Letter Race Game Cards

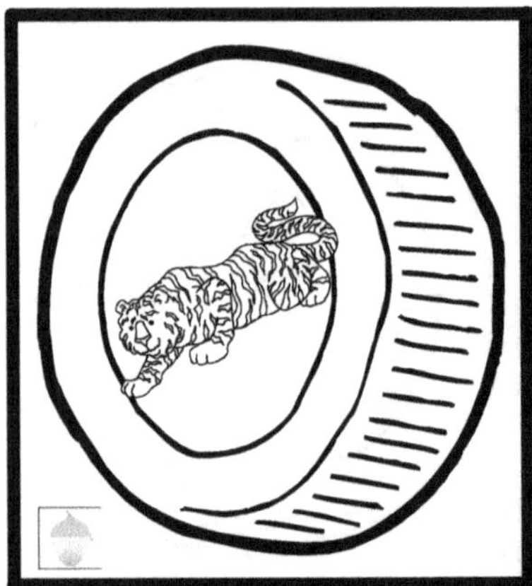

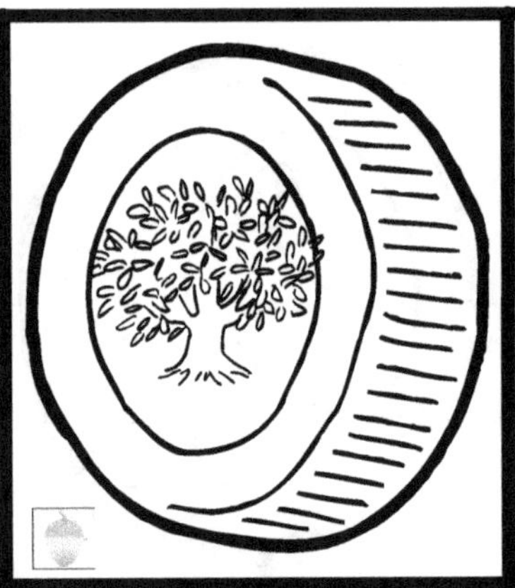

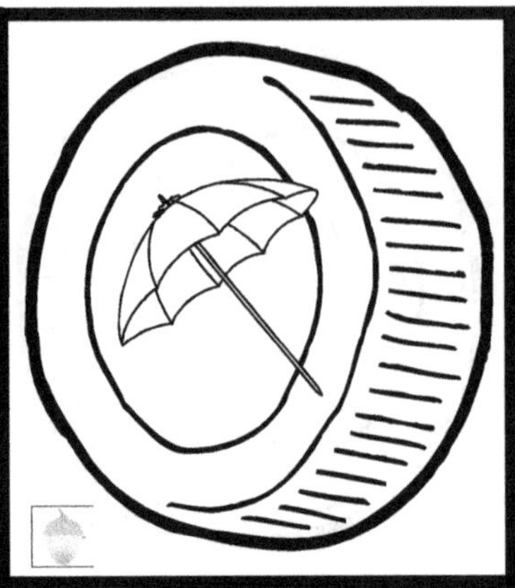

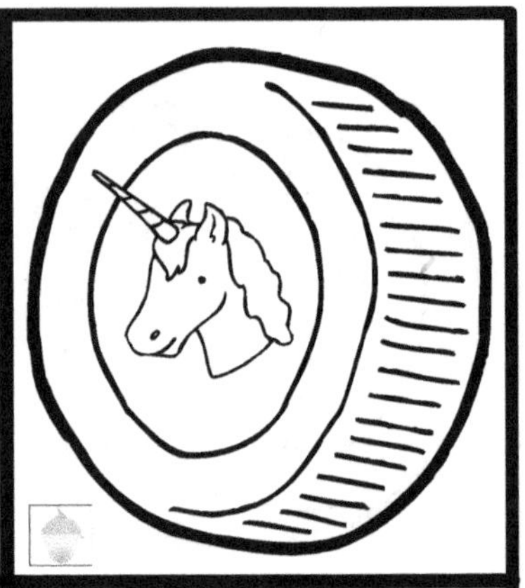

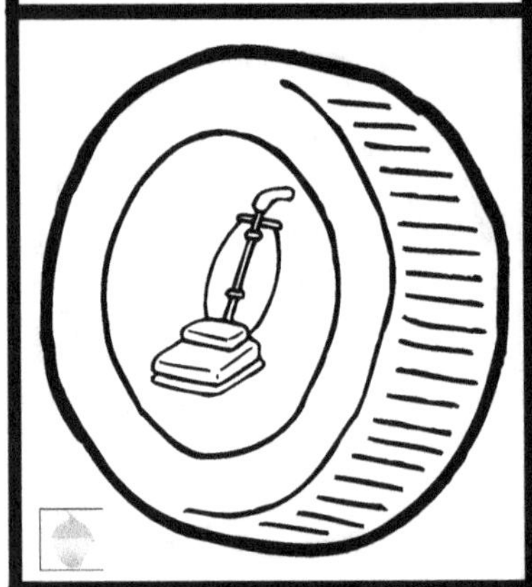

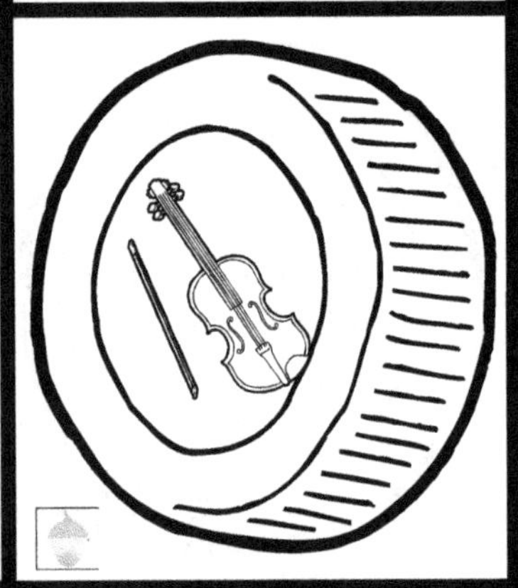

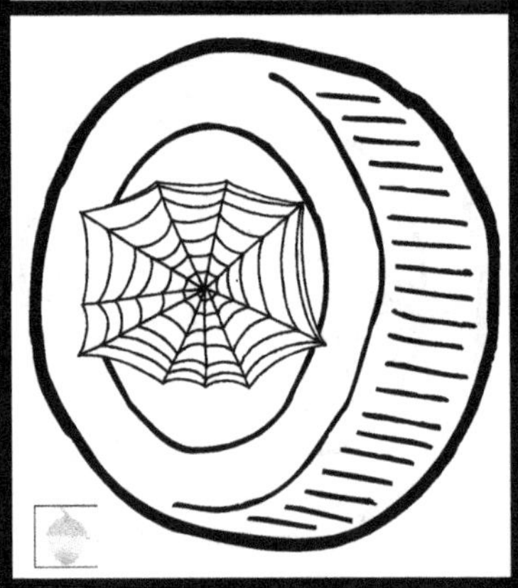

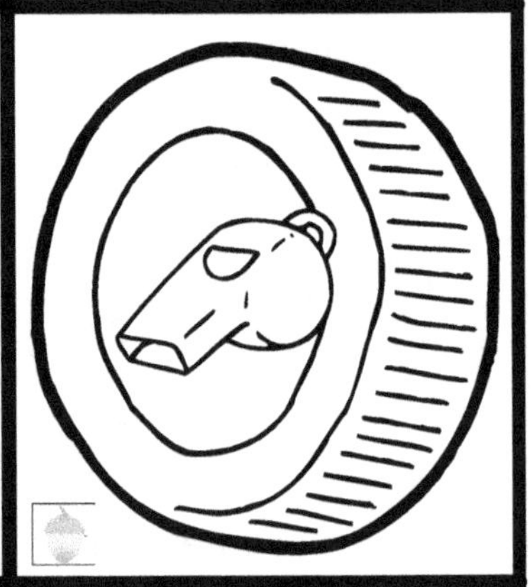

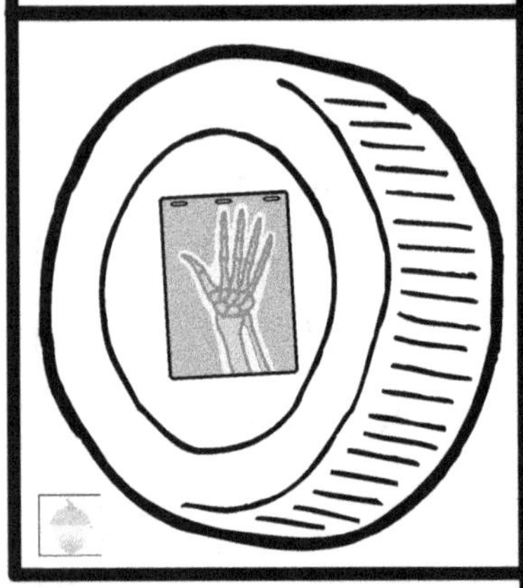

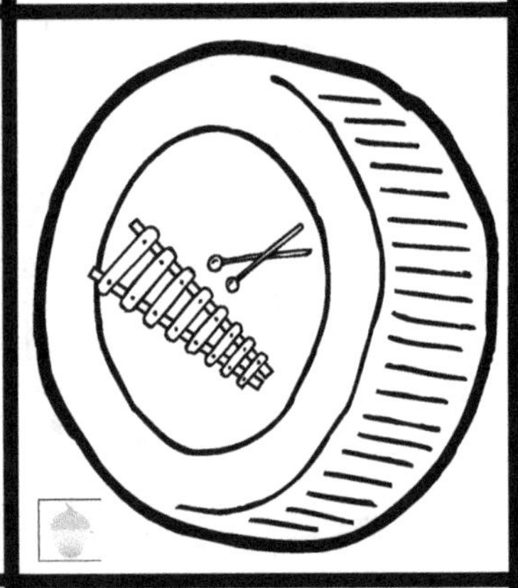

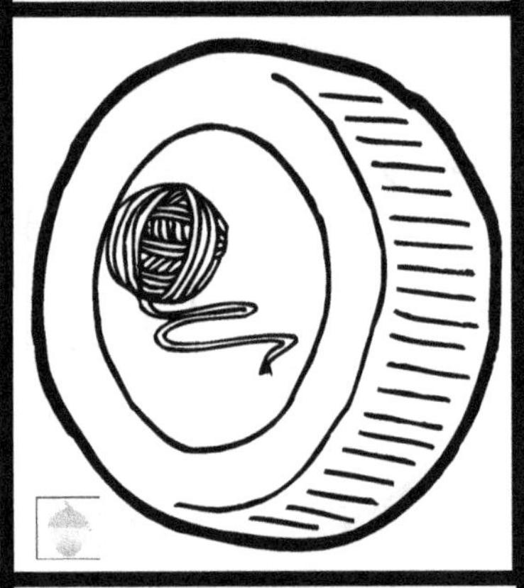

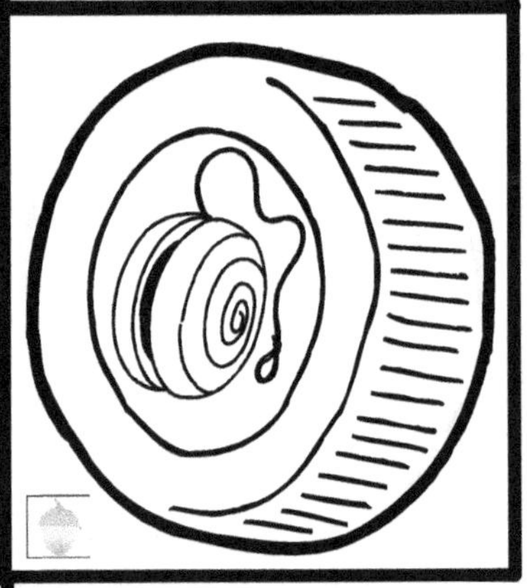

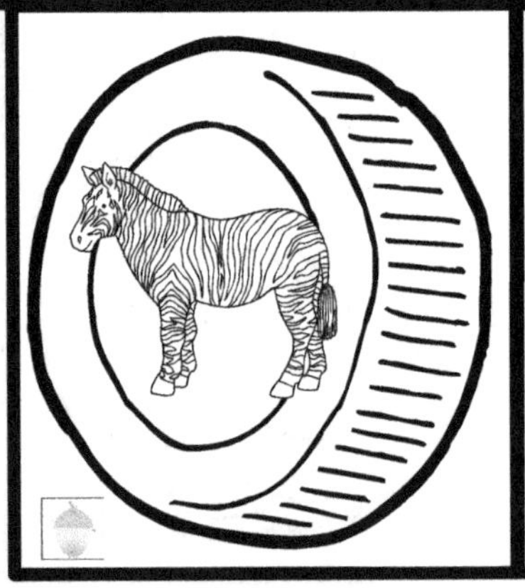

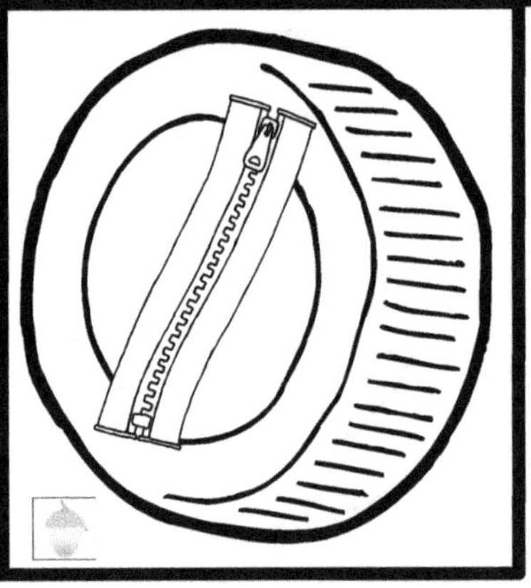

Awards Booklet

My Writing Awards Booklet

I can write my name.
_____
Name
Glue a flower sticker here.

I can trace uppercase letters.
A B C
Glue a flower sticker here.

I can write uppercase letters.
A B C
Glue a flower sticker here.

I can trace lowercase letters.
a b c
Glue a flower sticker here.

I can write lowercase letters.
a b c
Glue a flower sticker here.

Awards Booklet

I can trace numbers.

1 2 3

Glue a flower sticker here.

I can write numbers.

1 2 3

Glue a flower sticker here.

I can match letters to pictures.

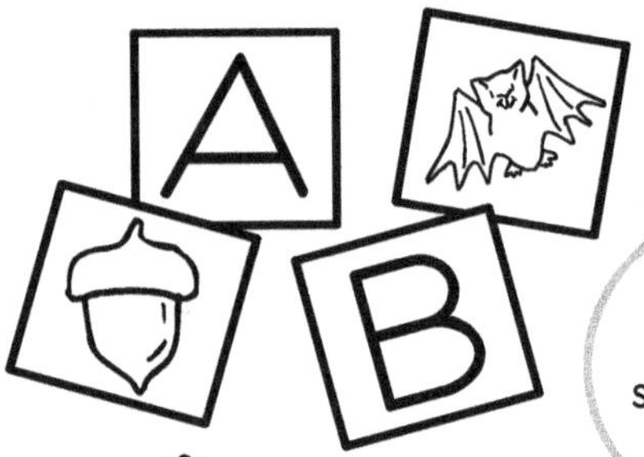

A B

Glue a flower sticker here.

I can recite the alphabet.

ABCDEFGHIJ
KLMNOPQRST
UVWXYZ

Glue a flower sticker here.

Awards

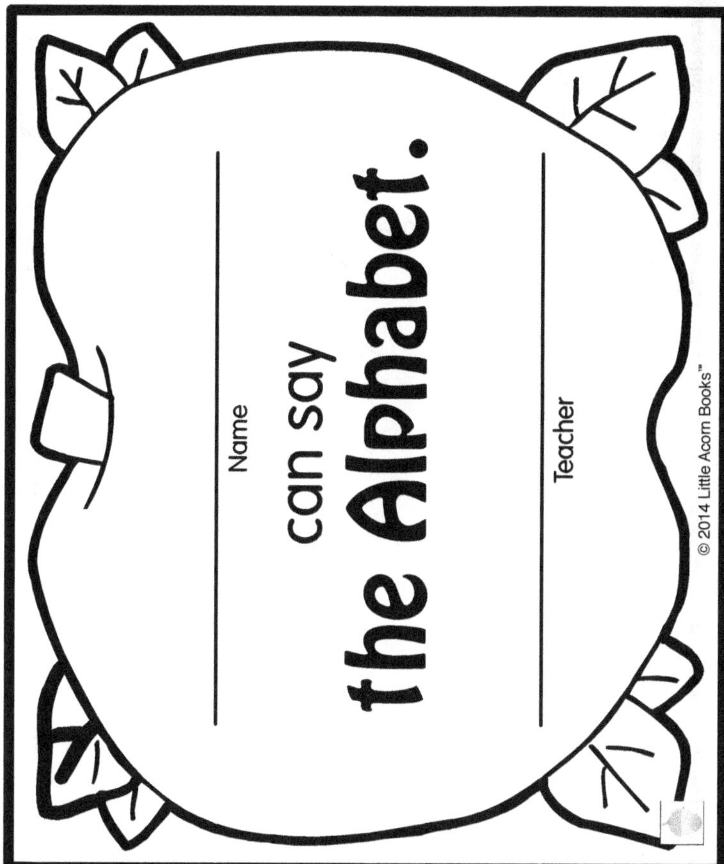
Name
can say
the Alphabet.
Teacher
© 2014 Little Acorn Books™

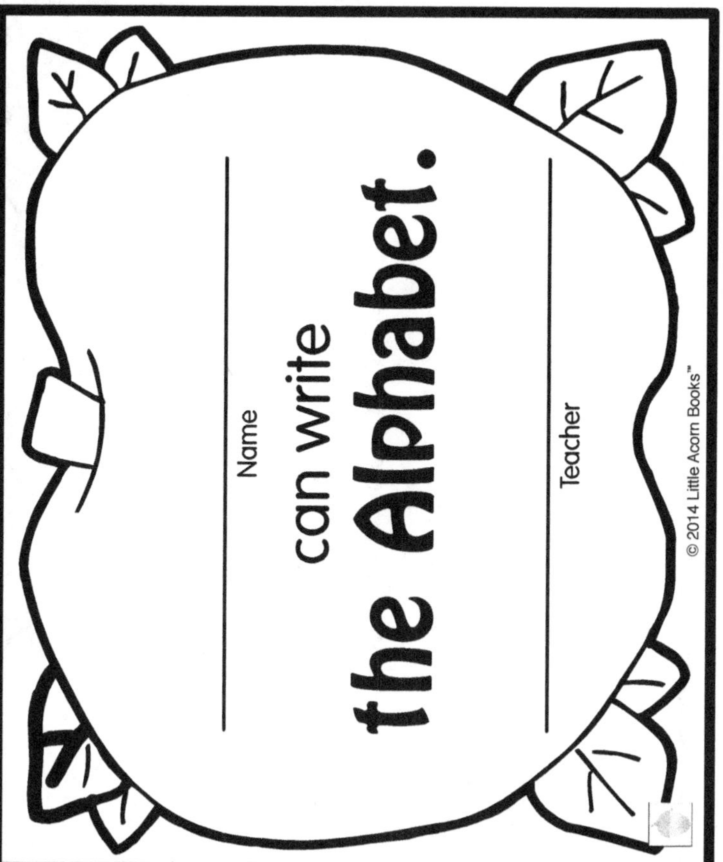
Name
can write
the Alphabet.
Teacher
© 2014 Little Acorn Books™

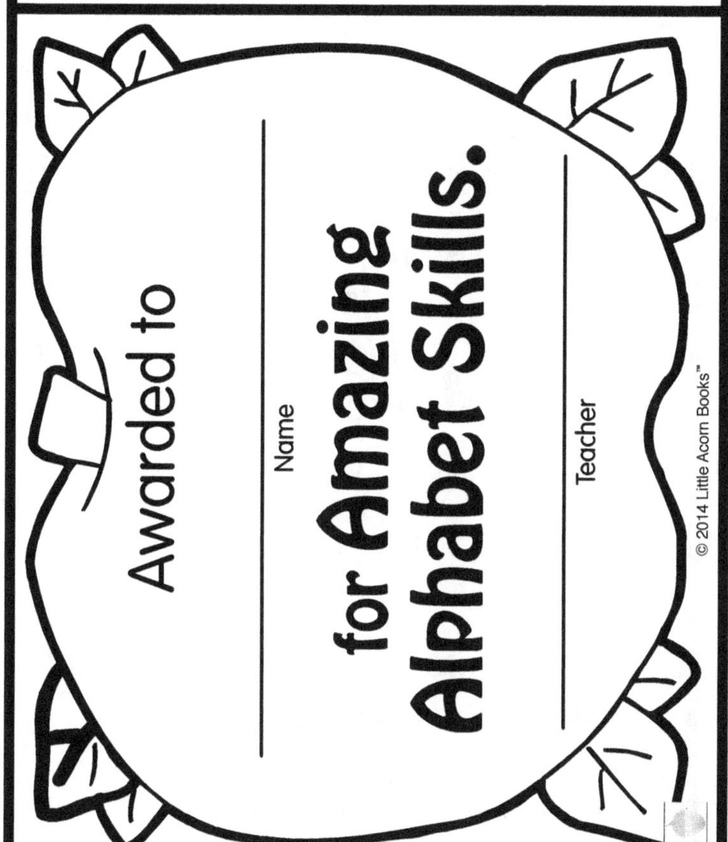
Awarded to
Name
for Amazing
Alphabet Skills.
Teacher
© 2014 Little Acorn Books™

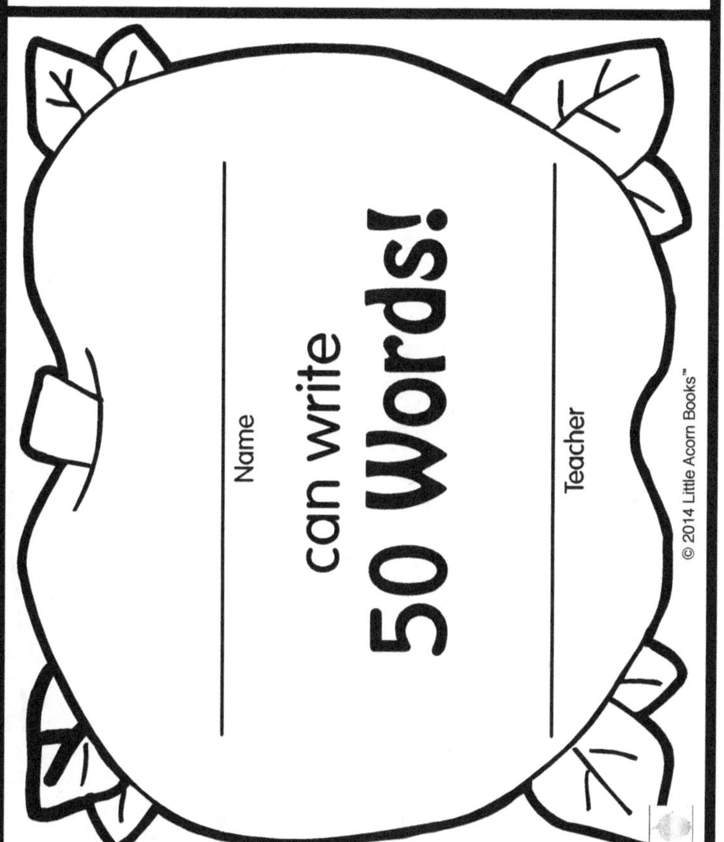
Name
can write
50 Words!
Teacher
© 2014 Little Acorn Books™

Take-Home Notes

Dear Parent,
We are learning letters. Please help your child identify objects around the house and write their names.

_____
Teacher

Dear Parent,
We are learning to write. Please help your child identify and write words for objects around the house.

_____
Teacher

Dear Parent,
We are learning about the following letters:

☐ A ☐ N
☐ B ☐ O
☐ C ☐ P
☐ D ☐ Q
☐ E ☐ R
☐ F ☐ S
☐ G ☐ T
☐ H ☐ U
☐ I ☐ V
☐ J ☐ W
☐ K ☐ X
☐ L ☐ Y
☐ M ☐ Z

Please help your child find objects that begin with these letters.

_____
Teacher

Little Acorn Books™
Promoting Early Skills for a Lifetime™

 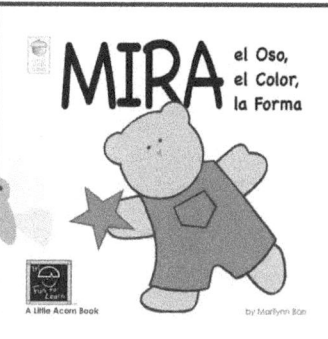  

A Hands-on Picture Book Series • Infancy–Age 4

Using Crayons, Scissors, & Glue for Crafts
Preschool–Grade 1

Miss Pitty Pat & Friends
Preschool–Grade 1

Mookie's Christmas Tree
For All Ages and Not Just for Christmas

Little Acorn Books™
Visit our web site:
www.littleacornbooks.com

www.ingramcontent.com/pod-product-compliance
Lightning Source LLC
Chambersburg PA
CBHW081020040426
42444CB00014B/3291